BILLY THE GOAT'S
TALES OF TWO TOWNS

By L. D. R.

BILLY THE GOAT'S
TALES OF TWO TOWNS

By L. D. R.

Selected Columns, 1949-1976

Luther David Ralph

Edited by Annelle Ralph Hawkins Huggins

authorHOUSE®

AuthorHouse™
1663 Liberty Drive
Bloomington, IN 47403
www.authorhouse.com
Phone: 1-800-839-8640

First published by AuthorHouse   08/04/2011

ISBN: 978-1-4634-4170-8 (sc)
ISBN: 978-1-4634-4169-2 (ebk)

Library of Congress Control Number: 2011913169

Printed in the United States of America

Any people depicted in stock imagery provided by Thinkstock are models, and such images are being used for illustrative purposes only.
Certain stock imagery © Thinkstock.

This book is printed on acid-free paper.

Because of the dynamic nature of the Internet, any web addresses or links contained in this book may have changed since publication and may no longer be valid. The views expressed in this work are solely those of the author and do not necessarily reflect the views of the publisher, and the publisher hereby disclaims any responsibility for them.

CONTENTS

A LETTER HOME..7

TALES OF TWO TOWNSBY BILLY THE GOAT
    1949...9
    1950...17
    1951–1952..23
    1953...25
    1954...35
    1955...43
    1956...49
    1957...51
    1958...59
    1959...61
    1960...65
    1961...71
    1962...79
    1963...87
    1964...93
    1965...95
    1966...101
    1967...111
    1968...131
    1969...139
    1970...149
    1971...151
    1972...161
    1973...169
    1974...177
    1975...185
    1976...197

A DAUGHTER'S GIFT..201

MEMORIES OF GRANDDADDY 203

LUTHER DAVID RALPH, AKA "BILLY THE GOAT"...........................206

I will lift up mine eyes unto the hills, from whence cometh my help.

Psalms 121: 1

The Holy Bible (King James Version)

With loving memories of,

Luther David Ralph (1890-1979)
Hester Carleen Martin Ralph (1898-1980)
Edith Carleen Ralph (1919-1985)
Mary Onezima Ralph Bradley (1923-2009)
Evelyne Lucille Ralph Harmon (1924-2011)

With love for,

Vivette Juanita Ralph Hawkins (1920-)
Luther David Ralph, Jr. (1921-)
James Tyree Ralph (1926-)
Mina Olivia Ralph Smith (1932-)
Benito Hester (Deba) Ralph Gammons (1933-)
Wallace Danley Ralph (1935-)

With a daughter's love and gratitude,
Tom Gilliam Hawkins (1921-2008)

PREFACE

Luther David Ralph was born on November 20, 1890 in a log cabin in Sumner County, Tennessee. The area was known as Shackle Island, on Long Hollow Pike, not quite halfway between Goodlettsville and Gallatin. His parents were Effie Gilliam and John Lafayette Ralph. He was the oldest of 12 children. (Luther's great-great-grandfather, John McMurtry, was recognized in 1947 by the Daughters of the American Revolution as the soldier from the furthermost west to fight in the American Revolution. It is said he came to Middle Tennessee, claimed his land and built a cabin then walked back to Virginia to join the Continental Army. Luther's grandfather fought with the Confederate Army and was wounded at the Battle of Shiloh.)

Family story states that Luther found the family home becoming crowded after the birth of the 4th sibling and so announced that he was moving out to live with his grandparents, whose house was just across the road. This was early evidence that Luther was "his own person," sometimes defined as stubborn by his own grown-children.

Luther started school at the Old Patton Schoolhouse on Madison Creek Road between Goodlettsville and Shackle Island. He then moved to St. Francis School which was in "downtown" Shackle Island. He often spoke and wrote of the headmaster who was his favorite teacher at St. Francis School, Mr. D. A. Montgomery. His grandparents helped him to continue his schooling at the Winthrop Academy in Nashville. After he finished school Luther became a "runner" for the First National Bank in Nashville. Then the wanderlust hit and in 1912 he and a cousin boarded a train to Chicago and then west to Colorado—where the "frontier" was filled with cowboys, Indians, and Mexicans. It was as Luther boarded the train in Gallatin headed for Chicago, that he had a conversation with the editor of the Gallatin paper. The editor told Luther to write him a letter about Colorado and he would publish it in the newspaper. This was Luther's first column. The letter was dated January 10, 1913 written from Stone City, Colorado.

Luther stayed in Colorado not quite 3 years and then headed back home to Long Hollow. During the ensuing years he married Hester Martin in 1917 and between 1919 and 1935 they had 9 children—2 girls, a boy; 2 girls, a boy; 2 girls, a boy. (Hester and Luther were married for 62 years at the time of Luther's death on November 22, 1979, setting the standard for their children, as 5 of the 9 children would have marriages that lasted 50+ years!)

Luther farmed (raising tobacco and strawberries), loved his fruit trees, and always had a huge garden to feed his family. He was a carpenter by trade, building houses and barns and furniture. During World War II Luther spent many months in Oak Ridge, Tennessee helping build the "mystery town." He actually developed a design for building porch steps that was later replicated on many houses built in Madison, Tennessee just after World War II.

In 1949 the editor of the new local paper—*Goodlettsville Gazette*—having heard Luther tell many stories about the region over the years, asked him to write a column for the first edition of the newspaper. Thus started 28 years (the last column was written in 1976) of "Billy the Goat's Tales of Two Towns" in that weekly newspaper. (While the masthead of the *Goodlettsville Gazette* did change at times during those years (including the name *Gazette & Star News*) it was locally known as *The Gazette.)*

I was two years old when Granddaddy began writing his column, and I have vivid memories of seeing him at the wooden table on the screened-in back porch of the house on "Vertical Plains" (the name he gave to his farm, because he always said "you can see forever on Long Hollow Pike, just look straight-up."). He would be writing his column using a pencil on tablet paper, or any paper he could find. The topics of his columns included current events; memories of his life on Long Hollow; stories of his adventures in The West; and, occasionally, columns about family events.

In 2005 I began a project to collect these columns and transcribe them into electronic format for historical preservation. (The University of Memphis awarded me a one semester Faculty Development Leave at the outset of the project, which allowed me to dedicate my work time to the initiation of this project.) Since 2005 I have located over 800 columns, many in the original newspapers and clippings saved by family members over the years and then more in the newspaper microfilm collection at the Tennessee State Library and Archives. (During my research, I found several other articles published prior to 1949 and I continue to search earlier newspapers published in Gallatin and Goodlettsville for additional articles.) Transcribing the columns—at this point over 200 columns have been transcribed—soon morphed into choosing some favorite columns to publish in print format. Luther's youngest daughter, Deba Ralph Gammons, supported my efforts toward publication and to her I offer my deep appreciation for her patience and love as I completed this book.

As could be expected, Luther did repeat stories over the years and some repetition will be found in the columns presented in this book. I chose to not edit out any of the repetition because each story would always support the general theme of that particular column.

At the close of the columns chosen for this book, a column published on December 17, 1964 is presented. This column was ghost-written by Luther's third daughter, Mary Onezima Ralph Bradley, in homage to "Billy the Goat." In future years my Aunt Onezima would write stories of her own, some of which were published in various collections. Following that column two grandchildren, both published authors, present "Memories of Granddaddy." I don't know where Luther's storytelling ability originated, but I do know it appears in the two succeeding generations and, perhaps, there is a third generation storyteller waiting in the wings.

Over the last six years I've come to know the MAN that I called Granddaddy. I count myself and my cousins extremely lucky to have these written words from our grandfather and to be able to read in his own words his love for his wife, his family, his heritage, and his "hills of Long Hollow."

Annelle Ralph Hawkins Huggins
Associate Dean of University Libraries
The University of Memphis
Memphis, Tennessee

Third grandchild of Luther and Hester Ralph
Daughter of Tom Gilliam and Vivette Juanita Ralph Hawkins

Permission to reprint these columns was granted by Ellen Leifield, President & Publisher, The TENNESSEEAN, and Interstate Group Vice President, Gannett, Co., Inc., January 3, 2006.

A LETTER HOME

Stone City Colorado
January 10, 1913

Published January 23, 1913 in the SUMNER COUNTY NEWS, Gallatin, TN

Dear Editor:

As the hills and valleys of old Sumner County hold a tender spot in my memory, the thoughts of which are ever causing that familiar song "Home Sweet Home" to buzz incessantly in my ears, I take this privilege of sending a letter home.

Only a few short months ago, back in Tennessee, among all the grandeur and greatness of that wonderful place, a friend and I became possessed with a desire to see some of the glories that lay beyond the "Father of Waters." So hoping that our ambitions might be realized, we packed our grips and set out for the "Far West"—at least it seemed "far" to us as we had never been out of Sumner County and knew nothing . . . . other than Sumner County and knew not but what the World was only a small space and our home county the biggest end of it. When we got to Nashville we thought it was some town, but on reaching Chicago, we were amazed, and but for the aid of a friendly policeman we might have been there yet, trying to find our way out. Luck, though, seemed to have been with us, so after spending the day in seeing sights we never dreamed of, much less thought possible, we found ourselves aboard a train bound westward. For two nights and days we traveled onward, never once thinking of the great distance that was being placed between us and home.

At last the train pulled into a little newly settled mining town, which not a year before was as devoid of human life as the Polar regions. Here we alighted and naturally the first thing, looked back to see how far we were from home, but all that met our gaze was the endless prairies and solemn mountains that stretched on and on to meet others in the distance. Lounging leisurely in front of the little station where we got off were a couple of big burly looking miners and they immediately sized us up, one remarking to the other, "a couple of tenderfoots."

The place we found to be inhabited by all kinds of people from all parts of the World, though we, it seemed were the only ones that had ever ventured in from Sumner County, or even Tennessee.

That night a dance was pulled off and after some effort we mustered up courage and went, and a lively crowd we found present. After a few minutes a fellow dressed in the attire of a cowboy approached me with a mischievous smile on his face and said, "lad get out here and dance." I thanked him, but begged to be excused as I knew nothing of the art of dancing, but he insisted and as he kept his hand a little too near a big six shooter hanging at this side, I decided the best policy for me was to dance. Well, I would have made it all right though it was my first time . . . it came my turn to swing and they would swing me a half dozen times more than they would the other fellows. The result of this was the first thing I knew the floor was spinning around and around, the next I was standing on my head in the middle of it, and there was a panic among the women in a struggle to give me more room. I found out afterwards that they were first initiating me and cared no more about dancing with me than they did with the boys of the Plains. Since that momentous dance, I have been "one of the boys" and have helped to introduce into our midst many other poor unsuspecting "devils" who have followed on our trail. The climate here, like the people, is quite different from that of Tennessee, the wind blows like fury all the time, and on account of this I learned that the chicken industry is a complete failure and the price of eggs too high to mention. The trouble is the wind blows so hard that as fast as feathers grow out on the chickens it blows them off, consequently they freeze to death, for the temperature is not nearly so warm here as it is in "Dixie."

The town sages say they are expecting cold weather real soon, it is twenty six below zero now, but they claim that isn't very cold for this country.

Wishing all my friends a Happy New Year and the Sumner County News much success.

I am yours truly,
L. D. Ralph

September 8, 1949
Goodlettsville Gazette

Tales of Two Towns
By Billy the Goat

This column will start in Shackle Island and eventually wind up in Goodlettsville.

You who don't know, Shackle Island is located in Sumner County at the exact spot where the buffalo trail through Long Hollow crosses Drake's Creek. And, that by the way, is the same spot the Yankee gunboat came to during the Civil War. We will tell more about the gunboat in a later issue. Goodlettsville, as you know, is the opposite terminus of said trail.

To make this column more readable, we will endeavor to mingle news of the past as handed down for posterity with amusing events of today.

We make no claim that Shackle Island is any better place to live than elsewhere, but do say its inhabitants are all good people. Not one of them would stoop to take anything that did not belong to him unless it was something he could eat on the spot and thereby destroy the evidence.

If anyone thinks that the Shackle Islander's appetite is being misrepresented, there is ample proof that this very summer a fellow, who is one hundred per cent closer kin to the writer of this column than twin brothers, went over to his orchard and picked a bushel of Roman Beauty apples. A rain ran him home minus the apples. When he went back, the apples were gone, but the tow sack they were in was neatly folded right where he left it. The taker, of course, could not eat the sack.

It has been a half century since an individual in this neck of the woods was arrested for stealing. Fifty odd years ago in the northern suburbs of Shackle Island, Sheriff Tobe Dodd called a man out from the breakfast table and arrested him for stealing a horse. Waiting on the porch, the sheriff allowed the fellow to go back in the house to change shoes. Inside the fellow put on his wife's shoes also her dress and sunbonnet. The milk pail in hand he stepped out by the sheriff with a polite, "Good morning, Mr. Dodd," and sauntered off across the cow pasture to a thicket where he mounted the horse and rode away.

The next morning at his owner's barn many miles away the horse was nickering for his rations.

Shackle Island has long been a baseball center. Now we have the school ground lighted and play ball most every night. The other night a record play was made. The girl's team played against the older men. Joe Harrison, the caretaker of the school, who had learned to play by watching the children, was on second. Norman Carruthers was on third. Joe saw a chance to come home and he came leaving Norman still on third.

The fellow who takes the cake for being honest is Tom Williams, who moved here years ago.

A short while ago Tom discovered in a twinkling of an eye that he had turned out to be an honest man. He was in Moncrief's Carpenter Shop stooped over picking up nails off the floor. Suddenly, he raised up and said to the man in charge, "Is it all right for me to pick up some of those nails?" "I suppose it is," was the laconic reply, "you have been doing it for the last twenty years and this is the first time you ever asked."

This column will use no one's name except that of a friend. However, one good friend, who has spent a lot of his money for cigars and half of his allotted time on earth at Shackle Island, has issued an ultimatum that his name must not appear in any paper. This fellow loudly proclaims the fact that he is the smartest man in Goodlettsville. Last week he told the company he is with that his brain is

9

worth $500.00 a minute to them. He even suggested that when he passes on they take his brain and picture and prominently display them in their establishment so that the "Billy Goats" that work there can see them every day.

It is obvious this smart man who doesn't want his name used has been reading the hand writing on the wall.

Just for fun let's see how many can identify this particular handwriting before the next issue of this paper.

Address your answers to Billy the Goat care of the GOODLETTSVILLE GAZETTE.

September 22, 1949
Goodlettsville Gazette

Tales of Two Towns
By Billy the Goat

Shackle Island has long been noted for its beautiful women and ugly men. They held an "ugliest man" contest this summer and about 25 men qualified in less than two minutes. However, Uncle Dick McQuick is reported to have been the ugliest man, with the exception of one, that ever lived near here.

It is said that back in covered wagon days Uncle Dick went to Nashville and was walking along the sidewalk while his brother drove the wagon along the street. A man approached him, looked him over and said, "My friend, if you will find me an uglier man in Nashville than you are I'll give you a dollar." "Poke your head out of the wagon, brother Mike," called out Uncle Dick. Mike did so and the man handed over the dollar and walked away.

Last week information was sought regarding the last name of Uncle Sam. Since then we have contacted Ed Lanier of Shackle Island, feeling sure he would know and he did, the name is Goodman. He says Germany twice learned that he is a good man physically after twice twisting the old gentleman's long coat tail a little too hard. And that most all of the rest of Europe knows that at heart, he is a good man because they get their eats from his Marshall plan, without mentioning some other countries that are aware of the fact.

You ask, of course, how this fellow knows so much about Uncle Sam. This is why: after living in 46 of the 48 states, he came here and married into a family that already had one teller of tall tales, who thought he could out talk Ed, too. He began by telling of a predicament he once got into, and how easily he talked his way out.

Whereupon Ed told of the time back in 1918 he, as a civilian shoemaker, was in Uncle Sam's army and of how he and two hundred soldiers were celebrating a little too much in front of the nation's capitol. They were arrested by the police and were about to be carted off to jail. At that crucial moment, Ed said, "Uncle Sam himself walked out into the street, informed the police we were his boys and ordered them to release us and let us go on back to camp nearby." So being the only one on record that ever saw the old gentleman in person, we are compelled to consider his advice.

Important announcement:

Kangaroo Court will convene at McCoin's blacksmith shop, September 31 to try and decide which it is—lather or sand, mixed with the Shackle Island News items.

Back to Goodlettsville with the story of George Lovett who grew up between two corn rows, and came over on the "March flower" from Sumner County. Although George sometimes associates with John Barleycorn he is a very likable fellow, and often longs for things on the farm. Last week he bought a jennet, patched up a stall and put a small tub in the rickety manger to feed her in. That night, after being out with John, he came home and hid his bottle in the manger as usual. Next morning the bottle was broken by an ear of corn, and the contents spilled into the tub and drunk up by the jennet. A little later the jennet began braying and kicking off planks like a legion of hornets had invaded her privacy. George ran and opened the stable door to see and out came the jennet staggering and stumbling, rolling and tumbling, bucking and snorting and shedding tears as big as hail stones all at the same time.

The neighbors all pronounced it hydrophobia, then someone found the broken bottle and smelled the odor—that told the tale.

George looked at the cavorting jennet a minute then said half to himself and half to the crowd, "Well, sir, if I look and act like that when I am drunk I'll never touch another drop." Here is hoping he sticks to it.

Moral: If the stuff can make a monkey out of an old lazy jennet, why condemn Darwin—a lot of others besides the jennet are still up a tree.

Tales of Two Towns
By Billy the Goat

November 11, 1949. Here is a thought for Sumner Countians who read this paper—has Sumner County degenerated in the last thirty-one years? Davidson County has a school holiday on Armistice Day, Sumner does not. Surely Davidson County children are not so much smarter they can get by with one day less. There is simply something wrong up the creek, for Sumner celebrated on that day in 1918. The big whistle on Shackle Island roller mill was pulled wide open and tied down while W. A. Dorris the fireman, stood by and fed four foot beech wood by the cord into the maw of that giant furnace. Men in the fields and housewives in the kitchen in several Tennessee counties and even in Kentucky, although they had no radios, knew the war was over because the mouth piece of the famous Belle of Sumner flour stayed on the air all day that day. Could it be that the Supt. of Schools, a veteran of that war himself, thinks Sumner county boys did not do enough to be remembered?

. . .

Well, Paul Revere had nothing on one of these boys from Shackle Island. He was passing through Gallatin on the train and learned the train was to be held there for two hours. He went to a livery stable, hired a horse and buggy and drove the twelve miles home, spent an hour there then drove back and caught the train. His mother who lived on a hill heard the hoof beats when they topped the first hill out of Gallatin and told the family she knew it was Walton for no one else could drive a

horse that way. Dan Patch made a record of 1.55 minutes for a mile. Walton Ralph made a record of 2.50 minutes on a twenty-four mile stretch. So let's observe Armistice Day in Sumner County if for no other reason than to honor that unknown horse.

. . .

Many years ago G. T. Moore lived on and operated a farm on Long Hollow Pike. On this farm Uncle Pent Isabel raised two or three acres of cabbage every year for the Nashville market. Good money was made in those days raising cabbage, but the cabbage worms were a thing that had to be reckoned with if any money was to be made. One day Uncle Pent was in town with a load of cabbage. While there a man sold him a box of sure fire insecticide, guaranteed to kill every worm in the patch, for one dollar. The box said, "Don't open until ready to use. Directions inside." Next morning Uncle Pent carried the box to the cabbage patch and opened it, inside was two wooden blocks with numbers on them. The directions said, "Place insect on block No.1 then hit him hard with block No.2."

. . .

Here is a human nature story depicting the personalities of a number of people with diplomacy panning out in the end. Cousin Gecrepy Ann, a fine old spinster lady, lived back across the country and twice a year she would stray out over on the pike and visit all the other cousins, staying a week or more at each place. She always came at turnip sallet time in the Spring and hog killing time in the Fall, and because all you had to do was set and listen to learn all the news, everybody was glad to have her come, except one old gentleman who had a large family to feed and felt she would eat him out of house and home. One morning this fellow, along with some others, was on his way to help a nephew strip tobacco. It being his unlucky day he met the old lady going to his home to spend a week. Well, all day he worried over her coming. Finally the nephew offered to tell him for fifty cents how to get rid of her without offending her at all. He readily agreed to pay it. "Go home and make her welcome," instructed the nephew, "then sit down and tell her the biggest tale you can think of, then tell her it is a secret and that she is the only one you have told. She will leave to go elsewhere to tell it." But the old fellow, like Washington, balked at telling a lie. "Don't tell her a lie," he was advised, "tell her you have just learned that $10,000 has been placed in the Goodlettsville Bank for you and that all you have to do is get a little piece of paper signed and the money is all yours. No need to tell her the piece of paper is a check for that amount made out in your favor and signed by the man that put the money there." The next morning the old gentle man came to work with a smile on his face, pulled a half dollar out of his pocket and handed it to the nephew with these words, "Here, you rascal, is your money, she left this morning before I left home to come to work."

December 8, 1949
Goodlettsville Gazette

Tales of Two Towns
By Billy the Goat

The writer of this column has been accused many times of living in the past. My accuser is a college boy who is president of his class and also a columnist for the college paper. All I have to say about it is; would life be worth living if we didn't have memories of the past to mingle with present day problems? I remember going to school but don't remember but one thing I learned. I think of that one thing always at this time of the year. It had so much truth in it I'm passing it on to you.

"Come little leaf" said the wind one day. "Come over the meadow with me and play. Put on your garments of silver and gold. Winter has come and the days grow cold."

On second thought I remember getting acquainted with three bears in McGuffey's old fourth reader. However I was not the one that ate up the little bear's porridge and slept in his bed; that was a little girl who lived in that old reader.

Now here is the amazing thing about this story, I never once thought I would ever hear of those three bears again, but last week just fifty years after meeting those bears, I received through the mail a gold plated fountain pen, also a ball pointed pen of the same caliber, and a fine gold handled pencil, so constructed all I have to do is turn a little gadget at the bottom of it and it sharpens itself. A card in the box said, "From the Smokey Mountain Bears to Billy the Goat."

One more thought, I remember, too, the story of three goats in that old reader, Little, Big and Middlesized Billy Goat Gruff who crossed over the bridge, the Troll lived under.

Now what I am wondering is which one of the three goats these bears think I am. I wish to express my sincere thanks to these denizens of the mountains for the nice gift on the fiftieth anniversary of our friendship.

A few quotations from familiar figures about town: Preston Swift reading the Gazette, "He came out and got in a Plymouth car." "Hat" on her way to the store, being eyed as usual by a bunch of loafers on the business house porch, "All you all do is just set down there and set." And now a boy who has never been to school and can't read but who is smarter than you would think he is. "What does that sign say?" asked the truck driver, pointing to the stop sign as he stopped for Old Hickory Boulevard. "Don't hit me," replied High Pockets.

This column has discussed the smartest, the ugliest and the dumbest man, now here is a story of a fellow that we don't know what category to put him under. The boys that worked at Tullahoma before they left for the army, tell of coming in from a picture show with Matt Williamson one cold night while working there. In the large room filled with beds where they all slept, they found Joe Ayers in a bed sound asleep. Matt threw the cover back and slipping his hands under Joe lifted him from the bed and laid him down on the floor. Then crawled in the bed himself and covered up. Joe says it is not so because he did not have any fight while working in Tullahoma but says print it anyway. Matt and the boys say it is the truth. Now with such conflicting evidence, the only logical conclusion we can come to, is that someone in that room, deciding he didn't want to be disturbed that night by a big fight, put Joe back in bed and pulled the cover over him before frost bite woke him up. Any way we nominate Joe the soundest sleeper since Rip Van Winkle.

January 12, 1950
Goodlettsville Gazette

Tales of Two Towns
By Billy the Goat

Christmas Eve at Shackle Island forty years ago; don't hold your breath, this one won't be about you.

On this particular night fifty or more men and boys had gathered at the two stores waiting for a Roman Candle battle to start, or some other excitement that never failed to transpire on these occasions. Awhile after dark two men in an open buggy drove up from toward Hendersonville depot and stopped in front of Worsham's store.

In the back end of the buggy was a gallon jug full of white corn whiskey. As the bright incandescent porch light glared down upon the jug, three boys, hardly old enough to vote, suddenly became very thirsty and it wasn't for water either. One of the men got out of the buggy and came in the store. Although this fellow drank liquor like drinking water, he was a fine man as long as you played fair with him, and not many ever dared play any other way with him, for that would have been like bearding a wildcat's den.

The problem that faced the boys was how to get the whiskey without getting caught. They finally decided to slip out back of the store where it was dark and steal along the bank of the creek to a vantage point past the lights, then step out and snatch the jug as the buggy came by.

Moving along on their mission, stealthily, one of them came to a big log (he thought). Raising his foot up high to step over the log he came down but there was no log there; it was the bank of the creek and down he went and landed in a big hole of water about ten feet below. An act of Providence no doubt for

that broke up the whiskey stealing and neither of the boys made drunkards, but Gee! that water was cold—I'm telling you. I am glad to add that the owner of the whiskey, now around eighty is the strongest prohibitionist in Sumner County.

. . .

We congratulate our good friend M. P. Frey for drawing the $150 at Moncrief's Saturday afternoon. Several others drew large baskets of groceries at the various stores in Goodlettsville that day. One such ten dollar basket of groceries was drawn by the writer, Billy the Goat, but somehow the word got out. Monday after Christmas there were twenty here for dinner. Some of them drove over two hundred miles to get here but they made it by twelve o'clock.

We all had a Merry Christmas, so who cares for "spenses" when they don't cost anything.

. . .

How many of you have seen the latest thing in writing material? When we older ones went to school we wrote the multiplication table on a slate, then wet our finger (by licking—ED.) and rubbed it out after the teacher graded it, then came tablets and now note book paper.

Everything reaches its zenith though. Now for the latest invention, they have reverted back to the old fashioned slate with a piece of sticky note book paper over it and hinged at the top. You write on it with any pointed instrument like a tooth pick or match and the words are plain as day, then you raise the paper and presto, the writing is gone.

However we learn that before slates were invented people multiplied on the face of the earth. (I understand they still do that—Ed.)

. . .

Goodlettsville has a lot greater population than Shackle Island, but the latter has a skyscraper and the former is minus one. The big five story flouring mill built about 1895 and rebuilt about the time of World War I belongs to Shackle Island. The present miller has been there more than twenty years. He is a fine fellow and very popular, in fact he is so popular that a town in another state is named for him.

I can prove this by the governess of the state of matrimony I am affiliated with. In July '48 we were on our way to California. The first night our train slowed up and stopped in a good sized town. I glanced out the window and said to her, "I have been telling you for thirty years that there is a town in Arkansas named for Mr. Will Herring, here it is." She looked out and saw the big bold letters on the depot reading, "Bald Knob, Arkansas."

April 13, 1950
Goodlettsville Gazette

Tales of Two Towns
By Billy the Goat

As the spotlight today appears to be centered on two towns other than the two this column is usually telling about. I am tempted to write about them. You can guess their names, after a couple of clues are mentioned. The first four letter syllable in one describes an activity that takes place daily and on a larger scale, weekly, in every home in this great country of ours. The last three letter syllable of the other town spells the source of a product used daily in every one of these homes.

These two are constantly at each other's throat causing them to make the headlines every day. One champions freedom of speech for more than a hundred million people. In the other town every last one of its hundred and fifty million people would be afraid to say "sooey" if the hogs were eating them up.

So it seems that the most logical and practical way to settle the difference between these two contestants is to split the difference between these two ideologies. This I know you will say is a very radical idea, the curbing of freedom of speech, but is it so radical? No, it's very sane, for the golden rule of every major religion including Christian, Mohammedan, Buddhism and Confucianism are identical in meaning though worded different.

They all sum up to this: Treat your fellowman as you would have him treat you. So why not let everybody talk all he wants to as long as he says something good about the one he is talking about. That at least would cut out over half the talk in this country and be a relief to us all if one was not allowed to say anything bad about anyone else.

I realize that as long as John L. is Lewis it would be hard for any of us to say anything good about him. But maybe a little sugar coating on that old tough shell around his heart would soften it up and he would let us have coal.

Of course it would be hard for Westbrook Pegler to say anything nice about our late President and his wife but at least it would sound much better when we read his column. It would be hard too, for the present administration to say a complimentary thing about the Republicans or Dixicrats but maybe they could if they had to.

Now, getting down to what we started out to say, if our papers and radios would quit picturing a vicious bear with a sickle of destruction and instead picture a peaceful teddy bear with a dove reposing on his head, we wouldn't be holding our breath so hard. Last but not least have it understood that a certain Georgian, not a native of the cracker state, should teach all his millions of subjects to look on and speak of our old bearded Uncle as a benevolent old gentleman like his twin brother Santa Claus. These changes indeed would settle things and the cold war would be over.

It would also be better for papers, radios and likewise grapevine back in the sticks to leave off all sensational scandal stories and talk about someone that has done something commendable. Well, if you haven't caught on, here is what I am trying to say. Let us all, both at home and abroad, be like the old lady in the story.

She always said something good about everyone never anything bad. So when she was asked what she thought of the devil, she said, "Well there is one good thing I can say about him, he is always on the job." Wonder if a big dose of sleeping powder administered to the old boy wouldn't solve our problems.

May 4, 1950
Goodlettsville Gazette

Tales of Two Towns
(no name)

Ever since this column has been running in the GAZETTE, three of the city fathers of Shackle Island have been "hounding" to have some of the virtues of their town extolled in here.

Well, to begin with, there is a close affinity between the two towns. In Goodlettsville the people are industrious and all work to make a living. On the other hand, no one, so far, around Shackle Island has ever even been accused of working. In fact, they don't have to work for a living, because, situated as they are in the heart of the fertile valley of Drakes Creek, fed by sulphur water of Tyree Springs, foodstuff grows wild in abundance, such as grapes, nuts, persimmons, apricots, Tennessee bananas and black-berries. All they have to do is go out and gather them and what they don't eat, they carry over to Goodlettsville and sell.

The fumes from this sulfur water make this place a virtual Garden of Eden, where things grow without work or spraying.

Sorry to report, though, that the last few weeks have been a near famine around this place. All the poke sallet got killed by frost, and that is what they all live on this time of year.

Funny thing, the last fellow who moved from this place to Goodlettsville got over there and found out he had to work if he ate, so he came back to the land of plenty and asked a farmer friend if he could cut a mess of poke sallet out in his fields. The farmer, not realizing how hungry the fellow really was, bade him to help himself. The farmer says that when the fellow went back to his car he had a two bushel sack full of sallet. He says further that he has been worrying ever since because he did not give the hungry man grease to season the sallet with.

Frank is the word, or perhaps it would sound better to say speaking frankly, we will not tell the fellow's name because there might be repercussions.

In conclusion, if any citizen of Goodlettsville would like a mess of poke sallet, get in your car and drive out to Charley Sandy's. The second crop is out now and perhaps the frost won't get it. Of course, don't bring an oat sack to get it in, but it would be well to bring along a couple of snake dogs and a can of chigger ointment. And by all means, as you return home, stop at Gus Worsham's store and let him give you a dozen fresh eggs to cook with the sallet.

Last but not least, stop at Irby Hutchinson's and he will be glad to give you a recipe book containing a hundred different ways to cook poke sallet.

1951 & 1952: No columns found.

February 19, 1953
Goodlettsville Gazette

Tales of Two Towns
By Billy the Goat

Thanks for the Valentines, one was a knockout or would have been had it been thrown instead of mailed. It was of yellow rock formation, the size of and identified as a petrified pound of butter. A little verse read: "Dear Billy, you old butter, you, Chew on this if you like to chew."

Valentines cause unexpected consequences sometimes as the following story will show. Here in this land of romance and intrigue where these tales originate there once lived a charming lady who for years had kept her cap set for a bashful bachelor living across the highway from her home. He sometimes came to the front steps and talked business and farming but she never could get him to come in the house or talk about anything else. She was fast becoming an old maid and pining her heart away, then came Valentine's Day and some mischievous boys sent her one to which they signed the bachelor's name. This valentine was full of cupid's hearts and darts and in big letters is said "Will you be my Valentine?"

The boys scrawled a note on the back with pen and ink, as follows, "When I whistle outside your window tonight please stick your pretty head out and give me an answer." That night she waited an eternity it seemed for the signal. Then in utter dejection, blew the light out. A moment later she heard the whistle, and glided to the window and hoisted it high. As she stuck her head out into the inky darkness she was thrilled by a warm and sweeping kiss across her cheek. Unable to resist she threw her arms around his neck, not the bachelor as she thought, but around an old horse's neck,

the boys had placed there. The horse threw his head up and started backward. Before she could think to turn loose she was pulled out the window and half way across the yard.

The next day when the bachelor came out to his mail box she was standing there with a dollar buggy whip in her hand, she flung the Valentine at him and started horse whipping him unmercifully. Unperturbed, he gripped her whip hand like a vise. Then picked up the Valentine and read it, "Unh Huh," he said, "So that is why my devilish nephews have been training my old horse to kiss them by smearing molasses and perfume on their faces and that is why my ink was spilled all over my desk."

By this time the lady was crying and trying to pull loose, however the story goes, he kissed her right on the lips before he released her and they were married a short time afterwards.

Out of pure gratitude, because he broke the ice, the lady fed the old horse a brimming plate of molasses and his favorite perfume every Valentine's Day as long as he lived.

April 2, 1953
Goodlettsville Gazette

Tales of Two Towns
By Billy the Goat

Hats off to the fellow who can appreciate a good joke, even if it is on himself.

So here it is just as he lived it and tells it for the first time with the understanding his real name not be used.

Bill Marathon, a well thought of farmer, blest with a large family consisting of a wife, a half dozen boys and some girls, last spring was confronted with a very complex dilemma.

Part of the family wanted to buy a television and part of them wanted to buy a new car. They finally compromised by buying both.

As the summer wore on it became apparent that the hay and corn crop would be a complete failure. There was only a fourth stand of puny tobacco and to cap it all off the bottom had fallen out of the price of cattle.

Now the big question that began to stare them in the face was how they were going to live and make the payments on the car and television. So a plan of action was finally decided upon by Bill to raise the much needed money. The plan was to set up a moonshine still, make a few runs and sell enough of the stuff to pay off the debts and then quit before they got caught.

Bill, when sowing wild oats in his youth, had learned the art at a clandestine college in the back woods country of Sumner County, where a fleet footed young dare-devil with a closed mouth and a keen eye could pay his tuition by helping operate the still. About a half mile across the valley from where this family lived there was a densely wooded section with an everlasting spring running in a deep hollow—sort of no man's land and an ideal place for a still.

Besides, the squirrel season was closed, it was too late for seng diggers and too early for coon hunters so no one would ever discover the still and squeal on them.

Mrs. Marathon, a jewel among women according to Bill, was bitterly opposed to this venture from the very beginning. However she never breathed a word against the plan for she was a woman that never argued with her husband over any of his pet ideas, she always let him have his way and trusted to providence that things would work out her way, which they always did.

The diplomacy, his wife said, proved a thousand fold better harvest for a woman than a ton of tongue and temper. So the truth of the matter is, this shrewd woman joined in with enthusiasm and helped formulate every little detail of the shady scheme, she even master-minded an elaborate warning system that would give Bill and the boys plenty of time to escape in case of a raid by the law.

Here is how it worked: about fifty feet in all four directions from the still this unassuming woman rigged up four cow bells, to each bell she fastened one end of a roll of binder twine. The other ends of the twine extended full length up the hollow, down the hollow, and up on each hillside. At the outer end of each twine she stationed her four youngest boys with instructions to each boy to ring his bell if he saw anyone approaching from his direction. Well, Bill and the two oldest boys worked hard seven nights and just before day the seventh night everything was in readiness to run off several hundred dollars worth of liquor the next night.

Then off in the distant night an automobile horn blew, the three stopped and listened. Suddenly the bell down the hollow nearest their home began ringing, they started to take to the bushes up the hillsides only to hear both of these bells start ringing, so with only one way left to go they started up the hollow and the race they ran would put any marathon runner to shame. Arriving home at daylight sleepy and tired they were afraid to go to bed for fear the officers would find them in bed and want to know why they were sleeping in daytime, so all day they worked along the highway cleaning out fence rows. Just before dusk they came in and sat down to watch the television and wait for supper and a good night's sleep. That day solely by accident one of the girls had moved the TV table over in one corner of the room at a 45 degree angle from the window and another girl had parked the black shiny car at a 45 degree angle out in the yard but about three times farther away.

Just at this time a gangbuster show came on the screen. Bill looked at the officers as they appeared and thought how thankful he was that they were on the screen instead of after him, but he could not help but steal a glance out the window and there to his amazement were life size officers walking forward between the car and the house. With a yell, "Here they come boys," he bounded for the backdoor, the two oldest boys following him. Well, to make a long story short they stayed gone three weeks in the woods around the still, got hungry and broke and ate up the mash. A short time ago they sold $1000 worth of hogs and paid their debts.

Last Christmas when the boys came in with three beagle hound pups, Bill said, "I thought your mama said you could not get them pups." Then the youngest one piped up and said, "She promised them to us for ringing the bells that night, we saw no one approaching and the officers you saw out the window was a reflection from the television."

May 7, 1953
Goodlettsville Gazette

Tales of Two Towns
By Billy the Goat

This may sound like a tall tale but it is written under the conventions of fox hunter lore which means that everything a fox hunter tells is 100 per cent true. However these fellows go in droves, so with a half dozen out together and each one declaring his own dog in the lead, that means a margin of 500 per cent can be untrue.

No one can deny though, that halfway between Goodlettsville and Shackle Island the topography of the countryside makes it a fox hunter's paradise. Three veteran fox hunters who frequent this happy hunting ground are Archie Martin, Claude Dickerson and John P. Buchanan, named for his grandfather and former governor of Tennessee.

Regularly these three gentlemen hike through the woods and park their lanky bone carts on a high knob in Bill Breezely's peach orchard and there they listen to the race.

Now the following story these gentlemen will deny, in fact they killed and dressed Bill's hogs for him and probably would have cut his winter wood to boot, to get him to keep mum, but Bill says it is too good not to tell, besides it is the only way he has to get even with them for the holes that are cut in his wire to let the dogs go through—so here it is.

One day last winter they were in their usual places in the peach orchard. The fox was soon jumped, but this time instead of the fox leading the hounds to Grafe Hill and on to river bottoms and back as usual, he circled around and around the knob in sight of them almost all the time.

Each time as he came around through a weed patch on the east side of the knob he would stop and wallow over and over until the dogs got near, then he would make another circuit around the hill and repeat the same performance when he again reached the weed patch. Each time he came around he was getting bigger and browner.

Finally after making a dozen circuits the fox stopped, turned around and began barking at his pursuers, the lead hound ran up and grabbed him, but no sooner did he grab him than he turned him loose and began howling like a mule had kicked him, then tucked his tail and lit out home. The next hounds did likewise, and the next, until the whole pack of ten hounds was heeling for home like old Satan was after them. Then calmly the fox sat down and picked himself thoroughly and trotted off looking for a rabbit.

While the other two were frantically blowing their horns trying to call the dogs back, John P. hardly believing his eyes walked down the hill to investigate, and there in a neat pile where the fox picked himself, he found a bushel or more of cockle burrs.

July 30, 1953
Goodlettsville Gazette

Tales of Two Towns
By Billy the Goat

Father's Day was lucky for me as the "kids" purchased the old goat a hammock to put out under the shade of the trees to relax on. It is not a stationary contraption, but has rubber tired wheels on it and all he has to do when he wants to move to a better shade, is call Harry Truman, the big English Shepherd dog, grab him by the tail and sic em in the direction he wants to go, then simply turn loose his tail when he reaches the spot.

You have been told that it pays to advertise, well here is the story of the greatest advertising feat ever pulled off in Goodlettsville.

Just 50 years ago this summer a fellow drifted into this town, no one knew from whence he came, who he was or whither he went, however, it turned out that he was a protégé of the leading store in town at that time. This fellow looked like a bum but on closer inspection he had all the appearances of a gentleman. For the sake of writing this story we will call the fellow Darius Dare, because he would not take a dare. Never knew but one other fellow like him. He was always ready to help on any occasion. Ask him if a task could be done, no matter how difficult it was even if it was catch a bull dog and pin his ears together without getting bit or drive a blind mule across a ditch where you had just stuck a hog, he would always answer with a vehement "yes" after first punctuating his answer by referring with a vengeance to a place much hotter than Tennessee has ever been known to be.

It is easy to remember the date this fellow came to Goodlettsville for that was the year that Sella Brothers and Floto brought their circus here. They put up the big top or tent down where the park is being built. People came from far and wide. There were more horses and mules hitched to wagons and buggies or under the saddle in Goodlettsville that day than there were people at the recent horse show or so it seemed to a twelve year old boy.

An actor climbed to the high trapeze in the top of the big tent and began swinging back and forth and turning somersaults. Finally after performing a brilliant stunt he landed down on the sawdust, in front of the great crowd and facing them said "I'll bet five dollars there is not a man in the crowd can do that." Away up in the roost at the back of the tent a voice answered. "I'll take your bet my friend." Everyone in the crowd turned around and began to stare to see who was fool enough to take such a bet. They soon found out, for Darius Dare came nudging his way down the seats through the crowd. When he reached his challenger there was a vertical bar about shoulder high suspended in front of him, he made several attempts to jump up on it and failed. Then with the agility of a squirrel he landed straddle of the bar and began pulling off his clothes, he pulled off seven coats and seven vests and when he started pulling off his pants the women began to scream and some ran out the tent. They should not have been alarmed though for when he had shed seven pairs of pants he was attired in a pink union suit like people wore a half century ago before the advent of shorts and arthritis. Then with a Tarzan like leap and a bound he was in the top of the tent, every time the other fellow turned one he turned two somersaults while the crowd cheered and yelled like wild cats.

But this story is about advertising. So just as Dare was shedding his last pair of pants the man that bet the five dollars with a look of astonishment on his face asked "Where in the world did you get all them clothes?" "At B. F. Myers & Son right here in town," was

31

the answer the crowd heard and since that day fifty years ago, the biggest portion of that enormous audience and untold numbers of their descendants have flocked to that store to buy their wearing apparel. Yes, they have depended on B. F. Myers & Son for everything from the first triangle creation they had pinned on them, to their wedding gowns and suits and on to yarn shawls and bedroom slippers that made them comfortable in their old age.

Well it seems there is a rush on in guessing who is who in those baby pictures but why not a contest you win "sumpin teat" as the old Negro woman said. So to the first three Davidson Countians that will call 5-2667 and tell in what way more tools in Sumner County such as hoes, pitchforks, etc., are destroyed than in any other way will be awarded a nice basket of Tennessee bananas each as soon as they get ripe.

Your answer must not contain but a dozen letters of the alphabet unless you are highly educated then you may use a baker's dozen but no more.

Next week's column will give convincing proof that the answer you must give is exactly correct. Please call after sundown.

December 3, 1953
Goodlettsville Gazette

Billy the Goat's
Tales of Two Towns

Owing to the fact that this story is more or less true, the names of the persons in it are all camouflaged.

The main character in it, if you were to hear his real name, you would be reminded of a weather shield on the front of every car, or else you would think of a gallant fellow from Texas who lost his rabbit foot in Tennessee, so we will call the gentleman Mr. Shield.

Until recently, Mr. Shield lived out on Long Hollow Pike. He was a fine fellow, but he lived in mortal fear of fast driven automobiles. He knew all the fast cars that commuted along the pike and also knew who drove them. However if one or all of the drivers had approached him on foot, he probably would not have known them from Adam's off ox.

The other characters that play a part in this narrative, although they are splendid young people, it is obvious that they would not care to be identified either, for it is a matter of fact that they have never yet been caught speeding, simply because there has never yet been a speed cop who had the nerve to drive fast enough to catch them.

No exaggeration—the cops chased one of the boys out of Nashville one night who played fox with them until he got through Goodlettsville. Then he hit the ground only three times between there and Shackle Island, that was when he topped the three hills between the two towns, and of course, when the cops got there, he was gone.

Now, getting back to Mr. Shield, he owned no car himself, but often hitch-hiked a ride to Goodlettsville, always with someone who never traveled over 40 miles an hour.

One Saturday morning last Spring he was on his way over to buy some groceries, he heard a car coming and hoped that some sane fellow would come jogging along and pick him up. Then he heard a sharp blast of a horn and knew it was "that lady driver" on her way to work. So in the ditch he jumped, just as she flew by. Then he looked to see who was next, and saw, like a colt following his mother, Tom Goryworth coming on his motorcycle and this time he jumped over the fence.

After the car and motorcycle had vanished over the hill and out of hearing, he listened and heard a mile or more out the highway from whence he came, the frenzied whir of an automobile and he knew it was Toss Robinson heading his way. In frantic haste, Mr. Shield spied a tall elm tree, 20 odd feet to the first limb, and started "cooning it," but before he had negotiated a yard of the seven yard goal up the tree, he saw and heard a shrieking flash of red and blue shoot by and he knew Toss and his two-tone was long gone again.

However, he was so badly scared by now, he continued climbing up and slipping back, climbing up and slipping back, until finally, although he had not reached the first limb, he reached a place that was comfortable and there he rested. Hearing the clickety-click of a Model T coming leisurely along, he looked up and saw an old friend with whom he had often ridden. "Hey there," he yelled, "wait until I get down out of this tree and I'll ride with you." "Get down out of what tree?" the driver said as he stopped "You are already down; come on and get in." Glancing down for the first time, Mr. Shield discovered he was sitting flat on the ground, hugging the tree for dear-life.

March 18, 1954
Goodlettsville Gazette

Billy the Goat's
Tales of Two Towns

I never like to write in the first person but in a column like this it is hard to write about the other fellow without somebody getting their feathers ruffled.

Therefore, this column has never amounted to much although it seems its consequences have been far-reaching.

I was asked by the first Editor of the GAZETTE to write something for the first edition. At that time I was associated with a very distinguished gentleman who was a wizard around mill working machines. I very often had to call on him to adjust a bearing on a saw, or line up a planer, which he always willingly did. The job finished, he invariably went by the office and told the boss he had been up to the shop helping that "billy goat" fix one of his machines. Anyway when this gentleman heard about the new paper, he dared me or anyone else to put his name in it. Under such circumstances I could not double cross a friend, who held me in such high esteem in the animal kingdom. So in the first edition of the GAZETTE this gentleman was fully described as one of the seven wonders of the modern world. Living right here in Goodlettsville, everyone in town knew who he was, although his name was not used, it was signed by Billy the Goat.

Now for the consequences, last Sunday morning when I reached for the funny paper, his picture was the first thing I saw. However it was in the magazine section instead of the funnies. Anyway, the GAZETTE was the first one to discover him and he is responsible for the nom de plume at the head of the column.

Goodlettsville is a fine place to trade. Here you can buy all the sundry necessities of life. Nevertheless in Dyer, Tennessee, down in Gibson County, you can buy "good money" for exactly the same price Crip Moore charges for "wildcat."

I have been played for a sucker in Chicago, outwitted the sharpers around the Blossom House in Kansas City and saw the sights in Hollywood and Reno, but the hardest thing I have ever been up against in my travels is pronouncing the names of the towns I passed through, forty-odd years ago when I was traveling through Iowa on the train. Sitting there looking at a railroad timetable, and thinking how far away from home I was getting, an old gentleman across the aisle spied me and asked "What town is that we are entering, young man?" I looked at my timetable and the town was spelled E U R E L I A. I told him it was "You reel ye, Iowa" and thought I was pretty good at pronouncing, but I had no more than got the words out of my mouth when the conductor poked his head in the back door of the coach and shouted "You're a liar, You're a liar." Then as he closed the door the porter stepped in the front door and yelled "You really are, You really are."

Now a word about Shackle Island. The people around that place have always been noted for their kind heartedness and their love for livestock. Farmers around there used to go to mill and carry a turn of corn and have it ground to make their meal. One March day, after a hard winter and a dry year before, an old farmer rode up to the mill on his old mare who was getting pretty thin from the effect of the lack of food. The old fellow had a turn of corn and when he rode up to the platform the miller was standing there and said to him, "Uncle Billie, what are you doing with that sack of corn on your shoulder instead of on the old mare's back?" "Oh," answered Uncle Billie, "I didn't want to make it so heavy on old Molly."

May 6, 1954
Goodlettsville Gazette

Billy the Goat's Tales of Two Towns

All characters in this column are not always fictitious. Here is a story that will show that truth sometimes is as odd as fiction. It is about a ghost town that, near a half century ago, was a thriving place just halfway between Goodlettsville and Shackle Island.

To describe in the burlesque vernacular of that era—"Beemerville, Shumbaker Street, Stump's hotel and nothing to eat."

One day when the owners of the mills were absent, the firemen and engineers of the two big engines started a blowing contest to see which could drown the other out with noise. One was a traction engine with a deafening wildcat whistle, the other was a boiler type engine with a whistle that roared liked a steamboat.

Anyway, they finally pulled the whistles wide open and tied them down, stopping all the traffic along the highway most all the afternoon, for not a horse nor a mule anywhere could be coaxed by all that noise and all that steam.

This town was located just over the fence from Aunt Sis' hillside farm. Aunt Sis was a fine old lady except that she sought to reverse the Bible injunction appearing in two different books of the Bible enjoining wives to be in submission to their husbands.

Aunt Sis' first husband died before the beginning of this story and she went to Nashville and found her an old Dutchman who had come over and hired to Uncle Sam to fight in the Yankee Army against the South.

It was a case of love at first sight when she discovered he was drawing a fat Federal pension so she married him right off the reel, bought him a grubbing hoe and brought him out to her hill farm and started him digging, not for gold but to clean the briars and bushes off her farm. She bedded him down in a little leaky lean-to on the back side of her house with two dogs and there, after locking up the house, she left him and went back to town. Oh yes, she came back to see about him the first of every month when the pension check arrived.

The Dutchman was a congenial old fellow who, because my father's name was John, always called me "little Shonny." One day the old man got sick and Dr. Buchanan came and said he had pneumonia. "Open the door boys, and put him in the feather bed in the front room," he ordered. Someone produced a screw driver and jimmied the lock on the door and in the feather bed the old man was placed and the neighbors nursed him. One of the dogs had taken refuge under the bed and bit some of them as they gave the patient his medicine. Doc ordered the dog be taken out, which was an exciting event as one bold fellow with heavy gloves on crawled under the bed and collared him and brought him out.

Luckily the old Dutchman got well and was up and about before the first of the month. When Aunt Sis arrived and learned what had transpired she was furious beyond description, but she could not afford to be too hard on the Dutchman until the check was cashed, so she went out and began to berate Lena, the head logger's wife who had attended the cow while the old man was sick. As Lena had done nothing to deserve a bawling out she picked up the hickory lathe, sawed from a spoke, shoved Aunt Sis down, put her foot on her head and gave her a paddling she did not forget for weeks every time she tried to sit down.

Aunt Sis had Lena hauled into court and Squire Jackson tried the case right out on Main Street while all the mill hands and neighbors stood by in orderly fashion and listened. Lena pled guilty and Squire fined her ten dollars and costs. Then the crowd got busy, someone passed a hat around and enough money was quickly made up to pay the court, with enough left over to give Lena to buy a new dress.

Now maybe you are wondering how the brave old Dutchman, who had crossed the ocean and volunteered to face Confederate bullets to free the slaves, reacted in this case—well, when he heard Aunt Sis screaming for him to come and help her, he grabbed his water bucket and rushed down to Ed Fraziers, a quarter mile away, to get a bucket of water. He was laughing as he had never been seen laughing before and shouting, "Ooo! I tell you Lena is giving her a good one. Lena is giving her a good one!"

July 29, 1954
Goodlettsville Gazette

Billy the Goat's Tales of Two Towns

What this country needs most is a good rain and an election . . . the rain to settle the dust in our fields, and make mud out of it, the election to dry up the mud in the air and make dust out of it.

In the case of rain, we might hope to get a few late roasting ears after it happens—in the case of the election all we can ever hope to get out of it, regardless of who is elected, is the fun we get out of talking about it before it happens—so here goes.

Everybody made up their minds who they were voting for the day their man announced, and nothing they read or anyone says will change them one iota if they are set in their convictions like the old scalawag who eats dinner at our house every Sunday.

Yet the NASHVILLE TENNESSEAN keeps riding Clement about his Cadillac. They try to make us believe that some guy gave it to him just for the privilege of hauling 40 to 50 extra sacks of beans to Tennessee, when everybody knows there has been a bean famine in Tennessee ever since the first Mexican bean beetle arrived. Why don't they believe what the man says? He says he bought it with his life savings. It is easy for me to believe him, for life savings don't always consist of money. Last week I read in the JACKSON SUN, I believe, that Frank used to hitchhike on weekends from Dickson to Erin a'courting. As a hitchhiker is walking part of the time, it is easy for me to believe that an industrious and ambitious young man would dig all the ginseng he came across in the wooded sections and old fence rows between these two towns and save until he was inaugurated governor. Stop howling

TENNESSEAN, if he sold his ginseng and bought the car . . . One fellow that frequents Goodlettsville on week days will still vote for him though he proves to be the champion ginseng digger of the world.

The NASHVILLE BANNER ran a cartoon the other day showing Browning robbing the blind by withholding social security from them without a mortgage on their property. We had a case like that up at Shackle Island a few years ago when Browning was governor. An old gentleman and his wife had raised a big family of children, all had married and moved away and were doing well. The old people owned a farm but the farm was run down and they had grown too old to work. They were in dire circumstances. The children had not been home in months because they knew there was nothing in the house they could eat or would eat because they had become too high-toned to eat cold water cornbread and poke salad. Still the old people steadfastly refused to ask for the old age pension because they wanted their children to get all their property. Then suddenly things changed overnight.

One Sunday morning the old lady was out in the yard and heard a commotion down the lane. Then seeing an array of cars and other vehicles approaching, she called to her husband and said "Silas, it is the children coming home for dinner. They have heard about us getting the old age pension."

The old people did not live long after this so, of course, you expect this story to have a sad ending . . . about the ogre taking the property away from these deserving children. It doesn't though, for the day before they applied for the pension, the old couple went before a notary public and made a deed of gift of all their property to their children. Browning will never live this pension problem down with some people, yet one fellow who visits Shackle Island on weekends will vote for him if he robs the vault at Ft. Knox and kidnaps all the soldiers guarding it.

It is quite alright for candidates to lambast each other as is their custom. It was started in Tennessee more than a half-century ago by old Dad Taylor, that good old East Tennessee Republican, when he introduced his two illustrious sons in their race for governor in the famous War of Roses. 'Tis an old story but worth repeating.

He introduced Alf, the Republican candidate, first by saying Alf had always been a good boy. Then he introduced Bob, the Democrat, by saying Bob had always been hardheaded like a mule. Bob thanked his daddy profusely, then turned to the audience and said, "Ladies and gentlemen, all of you here, of course, know what the daddy of a mule is."

Bob and Alf, who knew more about each other than any candidates ever did before or since, lambasted each other in joint debates as they toured Tennessee then slept in the same bed that night.

Wouldn't it be nice if it could be arranged to have Clement and Browning sleep in the same bed together each night after they make their speeches. Then we could all see this campaign as it really is—just a lot of bologna.

I suggest, though, that balusters be put on the bed to keep them from kicking each other out.

Billy the Goat's
Tales of Two Towns

Labor Day and we find the animals of the reserve seeing the Smokies after some never-to-be-forgotten experiences on their way there.

Joe McCarthy Polecat went by the way of Gallatin where he found they had had an invasion of grasshoppers, they being ankle deep all around the public square. He learned that polecats were making 75 cents an hour eating them up, so he tarried awhile.

Jonnel Lewis Coon traveled up the Cumberland as far as he could and then cut across the country by the way of Jellico. There he found coons digging coal for a living. Nothing suiting better, he wrangled with these coons until he induced them to strike for higher wages. But early next morning when the big Kern bread truck came by out of Knoxville he found the coons digging coal at the foot of the mountain, and the driver failed to leave the usual pile of stale pies and cookies. After a few mornings like this, the coons gave Jonnel his walking papers and went back to work.

Hairy Trumann Possum persuaded Mrs. Possum to accompany him on this trip. At first she was very reluctant about going along. Perhaps she was like the lady up in Long Hollow who visited the Smokies a few weeks ago. Before she went, she called her sister up and told about her sons insisting on her going with them, then she declared, "I don't care a thing in the world about going, though, for I won't know a soul when I get there."

Traveling strictly at night the Possums went by the way of Snow Hill and spent one day under the ancient Inn in which Andrew Jackson spent the night on his way to Washington to be inaugurated President. Nearby in Dekalb County, they found a sorghum mill making Warren County molasses and they feasted awhile on sorghum skimmings.

Frankie Clement Rabbit chose to make his journey to the Smokies by traveling along the highways at night and resting in the daytime. The car lights bothered him some but that was not his worst handicap. As you were told before, he was so called because it was imperative that he outrun everything else in the woods if he lived. So far he had been traveling over a week, wasn't half way there and had outrun over a hundred dogs. We find him just now coming into a town at midnight where the dogs are awful. They are running at him from all sides and he sees no way to escape. Then he sees what he thinks is a big truck pull up and stop in front of him, right in the middle of the town and he hears the driver call out "Crossville" and knows why the dogs are so cross. He runs under the truck for protection, but the dogs pile under after him he darts out only to find bigger and fiercer dogs waiting for him. Then he spies a compartment open on the side of the truck and a kindly man with a cap on shutting the door—so he hops in just before the catch locks the door behind him.

He rides and rides and rides and then the truck stops again and the door is opened. He hears no dogs so he peeps out to see what he can see. He is in a monstrous big shed with big trucks parked everywhere. One the side of each truck is the biggest, longest-legged dog he ever saw and they are all running right in his direction it seems, so he creeps back in and hides in an old suitcase with the lid partly open. Pretty soon someone comes and fastens the lid on the suitcase and takes it out and they ride again. Then it is taken out again and into a room where Frankie hears voices and smells cigar smoke, and he stays in there for what seems an eternity.

Now it so happens that the suitcase belongs to an old gentleman from the city who has worked all his life trying to get rich, until he could not sleep. The doctor prescribed counting sheep, so he counted sheep until night and day he could see nothing before his eyes but sheep, great flocks of them. The doctor then ordered him to the mountains for his health and said the mountain air would do him good. All day long he had enjoyed himself and was believing the doctor was right. Then he came to his room to retire, opened the suitcase and out jumped Frankie, who as he hopped out the open door, heard the old fellow say, "Drat that doctor and his mountain air, now I am seeing rabbits."

Once outside, Frankie found himself in the Smokies up to his ears.

Pretty soon he met up with the rest of the animals who had just arrived. However, there was a note of sadness among them for they all would have liked so much for their old friend Ike Isenhouse Terrapin to have come along. They all felt though that was impossible because the distance was so great and there were two big rivers he could not cross.

Listen, if you have a friend, never lose confidence in his ability to do anything you can do, for a moment later these gloomy tourists reached a shady spot and there was Ike, his head stuck in a half filled Coca Cola bottle, enjoying life. He had arrived the day before.

He had taken a bee line toward the rising sun and never stopped. The first river he crossed on the brand new bridge at Laguardo, the second he crossed over Ft. Louden dam at Lenoir City.

One of the crowning events of their sojourn in the mountains was a picture painted by Crip Chipmonk of the sunrise in the Smokies. The sun was so real it caused Georgi Groundhog to see his shadow and start digging a hole to hide in six weeks.

Eleanor Roosevelt Squirrel liked to play in the trees at Gatlinburg watching the sky lift go up. When she saw a New Deal Democrat and his wife board the thing with a bag of English walnuts, she jumped on them. She came back down, sound asleep, lying in the lap of Aunt Jemima, one of the cooks at the hotel, who had been up to get a "mossel of lung 'lixer."

February 17, 1955
Goodlettsville Gazette

Billy the Goat's Tales of Two Towns

A short time ago a lady from Lewisburg called Vertical Plains seeking information about another old Confederate soldier not mentioned in previous columns. So as a matter of record, that the lady may read, this one is about him. If she doesn't take the GOODLETTSVILLE GAZETTE she should subscribe to it at once.

This veteran of the Civil War, prior to becoming a soldier, was teaching school in Illinois. To keep from being drafted into the Yankee army to fight the South, he resigned and came home and enlisted in the Rebel army.

He was shot in the throat by a spent bullet at the Battle of Shiloh. The same battle in which his commander, the brilliant Albert Sidney Johnson, was killed. The rifle bullet, being spent entered one side of his throat and lodged in the other without coming out. Suffering great pain, this wounded soldier begged the doctors to cut the bullet out. But they refused saying it was impossible for the bullet to be there and him still be alive. When the swelling went out he placed the doctor's finger on the bullet and the doctor said, "Now we will cut it out for it will kill you later." "No, you won't now," answered the soldier, who at the age of 83 died with it still in his neck.

Returning home after being mustered out of the army, the defeated Rebel stepped off the train at Fountain Head, a stranger, and twenty miles from Westmoreland, his home. There a veteran of the Indian wars took him in and fed him, and there he met the Indian fighter's daughter, Millie Keen, who afterwards became the Lewisburg lady's grandmother.

This soldier, who later moved to Long Hollow, was Professor William Bennett Gilliam, the bearded singing master who taught singing lessons in Sumner and Davidson counties for a quarter of a century. In between singing lessons, with an old horse named Bill, he did a little farming and a lot of visiting around. He liked to mix and mingle with his fellow man.

Quite often, however, he did neither farming nor visiting on Mondays for about this time progress began coming to Goodlettsville. Two fellows there bought bicycles and on Sunday afternoons they would ride out the Long Hollow Pike. There they would find Bill grazing peacefully on the succulent grass beside the old turnpike, for then all stock ran at large. When Bill spied the bicycles, he would snort and throw his tail over his back and beat it toward Shackle Island. There the bicycle riders would manage to get around him and he would head back toward home. But Bill would never stop at home with a bicycle behind him, so on to Goodlettsville he would go. Sometime the next afternoon, after the Professor had scoured the country looking for his horse, Charlie Garrison, perhaps, would come along on the Belle of Sumner flour wagon and tell him that Bill was wandering around over at the Davidson County line. The old gentleman, taking the prank good-naturedly, would likely use his one and only curse, when he would say "Dog-bite the bicycle riders!"

As time passed Bill was superseded by a western pony from Charlie Wilhoite, who brought the first R. F. D to Sumner County. The Professor fed the old pony well and pampered her up, refusing to ever let his grandsons drive her. The roan pony, in spite of all her owner could do, would circle out to every mail box between Goodlettsville and Shackle Island. She soon learned where the Professor was in a habit of stopping and talking and she would stop at O. W. Kizer's gate and Mr. Charley Montgomery's yard and stand for thirty minutes every time, whether there was anyone to talk to or not. If the old gentleman threatened her with the whip she would raise up her hips like she was going to kick and one day she did kick him.

Now for one of the highlights of a boy's life. The grandsons were told to drive her and break her from kicking. Enlisting the help of another boy who could break any thing with four legs, the three of them hitched the old pony to the buggy and let her ease off until they got around the curve from grandpa. Then they stopped at the first buggy whip vendor they came to and got them one apiece. Yes, they had them then like they have soft drink and cigarette vendors today—any green sycamore stump beside the highway.

Here the fun began. The driver stood on the seat, out of reach of her heels. A left-handed boy stood on one side and a right-handed one on the other. She kicked only once. The sycamore tree was too hot for her. At the talking stops going up, the right-handed boy applied it, at the blacksmith shop the left-handed one, and vice versa coming back. She was not even allowed to stop at Shackle Island. A half mile further on she was turned around and came through again without stopping until she reached home. On the return trip the whole countryside was out looking for they did not think it was in the old filly to make the round in a record time that few automobiles have made since. Anyway she never again kicked the Professor and moved when he said, "Giddup."

The genial old Professor, whether working, traveling, or sitting at home resting, was always humming a gospel song, usually, "The Great Physician."

Living deep between the hills of Long Hollow, he always had a ready reply to all comers. One day a pompous stranger drove up in a buggy and stopped. "My friend," he said, "Does the sun ever shine in this hollow?" "Yes sir," answered the Professor, "every other day in clear weather."

Billy the Goat's Tales of Two Towns

Sixteen years ago, to be exact, the Long Hollow Pike, before they built the new highway, was like an old fashioned washboard.

The grader was run over once a month digging out ruts in it that looked, when lights of cars played over it, like waves on water. Midway in Long Hollow there was a high bridge directly on a curve where near a hundred cars had overturned. A fellow who lived near by and had often been called out of bed to assist the victims of the wrecks, had persistently urged "Sleepy" Harris, the road superintendent, to build balusters on the curve and paint them white so motorists could see the curve before they reached it.

Sleepy neglected to take the fellow's advice so in desperation he sent a protest to the GALLATIN NEWS ribbing Sleepy about the condition of the road.

Whether that had anything to do with it or not, the balusters were built the very next week and no car has ever overturned there since.

Mrs. Janie Montgomery of Shackle Island cut this old article out of the Gallatin paper and saved it and now wants it printed again in a paper because the new highway is now becoming full of holes like the old one was.

The present superintendent is named Parker, a very significant name in this case, for if the road isn't fixed before it gets any worse there will be but one thing for a person to do who lives out Long Hollow way and owns a new car or old one either and that will be to "park'er" and start walking. Hoping that Mr. Parker will read this as Sleepy Harris did

March 16, 1939, here is the reprint entitled *"Rough Riding."*

"Rough Riding"

Here dear public is a camouflaged line
About the grand old County the stork made mine.
We pay homage to its hallowed tradition and
chivalry
And the gallant sons on the pages of history.
Of fertile valleys and blue-grass hills we're justly
proud,
While in honor to old landmarks our heads are
bowed.
The landmarks though, the tourists will never
forget,
But always remember 'tis safe to bet,
Is winding through valleys and over hills,
The perforated Pike 'tween Gallatin and
Goodlettsville.

This road of course has many high points,
Like magic it limbers up all rheumatic joints,
For simple maladies like lumbago, colic and gout
A ride on this road will shake your ailments out.
Milk hauled on this road to butter turns,
So the farmer sells butter but never churns.
A sure panacea for all human ills,
This perforated Pike between Gallatin and
Goodlettsville.

In T-Model Ford geared with baling wire
Or riding in luxury in a late model car,

It's just bouncing along trusting
Providence
To keep from straddling some farmer's fence.

Once a moon this road is neatly combed with
grader
Encouraging cars to make twenty miles or faster.
Then brakes screech on, but stop they can't,
Where the perforated ought to be ahead, it ain't,
A misplaced bridge, oh save a soul,
As the car turns turtle in a ten-foot hole.

Yes, the ambulance, and a hospital bill
Haunts the perforated Pike from Gallatin to
Goodlettsville.

Surely there's a remedy, a simple sort of bitters,
To stop drivers on this road from having nervous
jitters,
To keep mules and cars alike from going along so
creepy.
Awake! Rip Van Winkle awake, forget that you
are "Sleepy,"
For twenty long rough years there has been ruts to
fill
On the perforated Pike from Gallatin to
Goodlettsville.

—L. D. Ralph
Shackle Island, Tenn.

December 3, 1955
Goodlettsville Gazette

Billy the Goat's
Tales of Two Towns

The quickest way to lose your socks is to start writing a column like this. A few weeks ago at the insistence of an immigrant from the Sixth District of Sumner County, there was an inflection made in here on the truthfulness of Green Newbern. Green took it alright, didn't get mad or anything of the sort. In fact, he was so nice about it that when he approached me last week and wanted to borrow a set of ribs and backbone until he killed hogs, I couldn't resist letting him have them.

A short time afterwards, I learned that Green had not killed hogs in 20 years and that there was no likelihood of him doing so in the next 20, which proves, if you play with fire, it will surely burn.

Last Wednesday night the girl from Vertical Plains that works at the bank gave a supper in celebration of Winston Churchill's birthday. All the children and grandchildren were there except the two boys and their families in California. They called us over the phone and we had a chat with them, too. However, none of them gave the old Englishman a thought that night, because he has no monopoly on birthdays. It was their Daddy's, too.

The first lady of Goodlettsville, who lives on Capitol Hill, was gracious enough to bake the cake for the affair. The cake was beautifully decorated—only one candle on it, which appropriately was a cardboard replica of a barnyard animal with a short tail on one end and horns and whiskers on the other. On the side of this pesky animal was printed the figure 65. Which means, of course, that a fellow is of age and can retire and draw rocking chair money. But not for me, it doesn't. My salary for writing this column makes me ineligible to draw it. True, it is only 51 copies of the GAZETTE per year. The catch is when they asked Allen Merritt how much the paper is worth a week to a subscriber, he will say not less than $25 a week and I am allowed to make only $20 to be eligible.

Well, it seems they have changed the golden rule at the Bank of Goodlettsville, not withstanding this fact though. People still flock in there to get change. Witness them coming out of there with red and green yardsticks.

Believe it or not there is one man in Goodlettsville that you can't even call his name without asking questions. The question is, will HIT? But owing to the fact that he has not played baseball in years he cannot answer the question himself. However, this man is an accomplished shoe salesman. If you go in his store for a pair of shoes and stick your left foot out first, he will invariably put the right shoe on the left foot, then pick up the left shoe and put it on the right foot. The amazing thing is, they fit that way and that is the way you wear them.

POSTHASTE: Dead Santa, please bring me an old fashioned Christmas breakfast of a quarter of a century ago, before the days of electric stoves, instant coffee, and fruit cake. With it bring the magic change from white beans and chunk meat, biscuits and sorghum molasses that went with it.

Yes, in those days there were a half dozen coconut and "Choconut" cakes baked out of Belle of Sumner flour and fresh boiled ham.

A little after daybreak on Christmas morning when the nine "kids" were out of bed and their stockings erupted, we would gather around the old wood cook stove to smell the aroma of a steaming pot of coffee and eat ham sandwiches and cake, for we never waited 'til dinner to cut them. And we had light bread that morning for the first time that year. Now it is three times a day we have it.

One other thing I want is a chameleon bedspread to replace the white one on the bed by the wood fireplace, so when I come in from work tired and lay down to rest, it will change color to match the tobacco crumbs from my pocket and the hayseed and sawdust from my clothes.

A strange request this last one indeed, but who wants to listen to a sermon when the preacher isn't licensed to preach.

July 12, 1956
Goodlettsville Gazette

Billy the Goat's
Tales of Two Towns

A Goodlettsville lady every time she sees me asks about television, this lady, using words of Mortimer Snerd, is "my kind of people" for she too, when she is looking at a program, can't stand being interrupted by someone butting in to tell about Sal Jones coming over to swap a setting of duck eggs or something else just as silly. Therefore, I am making this report to her on above subject.

This lady, I presume, likes March in August and enjoys a fox race very Sunday night. Well, she can have Hal March and Sonny Fox. I'll take the 64 thousand.

The thing that makes television so fascinating is the fact that it is not directed by mere human beings, but is bossed by a mere maid out of the ocean. Yes, they even have to get Miss Agatha's permission to smoke on the screen, then she runs and jumps back into the water.

★   ★   ★

How many heard the timely advice the young woman gave Groucho about the abundance of fruit we have this year? It was good advice and also shows the complexity of this English language of ours. She said, "I eat all I can, can what I can't, then later eat what I can."

The most sensible words I have ever heard spoken on our set were uttered by a wooden headed character, when Charlie McCarthy said, "Children should have shorter hours in school to give them longer hours to look at television." I heartily agree with him because that is where the children of this generation are going to get their education. None of the small fry today would know the Governor of Tennessee if he were to appear before their eyes, but every last one of them would recognize Roy Rogers.

I have just received word from Captain James in California, who sent the contraption here, advising me to stay off the hill and look at the television and relax. Listen boy, if you are getting a Ph.D. in Agriculture in a few weeks, haven't they ever taught you that watching television won't keep crab grass out of strawberries?

Besides the hilltop of Vertical Plains is nearer heaven than you might think, because when I work in Goodlettsville five days a week, where people look down on me as just a scalawag carpenter, which I don't mind one bit, remembering as I do that the greatest carpenter that ever lived found no honor in his home town, I then return home, take my hoe and climb to the top of the hill, where I look down on Goodlettsville four miles away and think how far beneath me it is.

★   ★   ★

Yes, it is invigorating to stand up there and breathe the fresh air as I watch Mr. Dorris milking his cow and see Allen Mathis when he leaves the barber shop and goes home to roost.

Well, Captain, I am under strict orders to write nothing about the family, things you might like to hear. However, one of the censors, a Nashville artist, cleared this last little story and said I might write it.

To begin the story, a few weeks ago we viewed an example on television of the perfect wife, in the person of Margaret Truman, blind-folded on a panel show talking to Clifton Daniels, her husband, without recognizing his voice.

I think now what a privilege that would be, talking to your wife and her not knowing

49

who you were, you wouldn't be told to go after the cows or to brush the sawdust off you before lying down on the couch to watch a program. Anyway it put an idea in my head.

★   ★   ★

For weeks, I practiced changing my voice, then the other day I called Vertical Plains from the shop and stated that I was calling to tell her that at that very moment that husband of hers was in Goodlettsville talking to a woman, then added that it was not the first time he had been seen talking to that same woman either. "Wait until he gets home," she exclaimed.

I then said, "Looks like a fellow with a wife as pretty as you are wouldn't notice any other woman," then I hung up.

When I arrived home that afternoon she was all smiles and began telling me about a real nice fellow, calling her over the phone. Then she began hinting about the nice things he said to her. When I began to laugh and she saw she was not making me jealous, she changed and blatted out, "That's alright, Mr. Smarty, who was that hussy you were talking to in Goodlettsville today?"

January 3, 1957
Goodlettsville Gazette

Billy the Goat's
Tales of Two Towns

Lest we forget before continuing about last week's activities, let's give thanks to the One that furnished His birthday for us to celebrate and let's remember the shepherds and wise men that visited the birthplace, thereby giving incentive to our own children to return home to their birthplace on Christmas Day.

They have all returned home now but they left pleasant memories and a lot of gifts with us. Twenty-one were present and eight couldn't get here. We also wish to thank you for the cards my wife and I received, hundreds of them from everywhere, even across the sea. However, some of the senders have surely been reading this column and came to the conclusion that she wears the britches here. They began arriving early, some addressed to Mr. and Mrs. Hester Ralph causing her to brag that everyone knows she is the boss. Christmas Eve though we received one from my old friend Joe Howdyshake over in Timbuctoo that set her back on her place. It was addressed to Billy the Goat and Nannie, Vertical Plains, Tenn.

Christmas started with us Saturday night with the Christmas tree at Old Beech. There you don't expect an expensive gift but you sure get a kick out what you give and receive. I gave a large ear of yellow corn, unwrapped to my good friend Irby Hutchison and also a quart jar of whippoorwill peas in the hull to our preacher, Ed McCoy. They got a big laugh but I knew my time was coming and it did. First, they brought me three stringy sweet potatoes entwined around each other in an inseparable Gordian knot. Next, it was a nice watermelon, but when I went to cut

into it it was a citron, and then a turnip that measured thirty-one inches in circumference and weighed eleven pounds. So you see why I give jokers, I always receive them up there and everybody enjoys them.

The most fun I had though was when the superintendent of Sunday School asked me to be Santa Claus. I told him I would be for the grown-ups if he would wear the suit and do the acting for the children. Maybe you think it didn't work but it did. The tree and the audience were in the basement. I walked out shortly before time for the old gentleman to enter and stood at the foot of the blind stairway and sang a Santa Claus song that I made up and sang years ago when I used to play Santa. Then I walked back up the steps and the man with the suit on entered.

Everybody of course knew exactly who it was for they all recognized my voice besides no one can sing as loud as I do making them doubly sure. A minute later though I walked in the front door and took my seat, which I had left a short time before. The crowd saw we had put one over on them and grinned sheepishly. After the program a number of people came around flattering me about how well I sang, as if anybody couldn't sing that could carry a tune and had nerve enough to open his mouth like he was calling hogs.

Only one fellow in the whole audience was frank enough to admit how he felt about it. He told my wife while I was singing that he wished he was at the top of the steps with a three gallon bucket of water so he could throw it on 'em. Thank you Irby, you are still your old self.

Oh yes, I was presented with many nice gifts at the tree here at home but to the most magnificent of all there is quite a story attached.

Several weeks ago when grub began to play out at Jack Givens he sent his wife out to gather persimmons but when she got to the tree they weren't ripe so she stayed until they got ripe.

Last week after spending a hundred dollars bus fare and staying away from home a whole month, she returned home with one persimmon. But listen, that was no ordinary specimen of possum diet she fetched home for it was as big as a large delicious apple and not a seed in it and taste, my goodness, it was good. How do I know? Well you see, Jack kept it a week or so and showed it to all his friends and then decided that a Billy Goat was the nearest thing to a varmint he could find to eat it so he sent it down to me. Incidentally, this persimmon grew in Jack's grandson's yard in Palo Alto, California. It was growing there long before the little fellow was born and, by the way, he is my grandson too. Thank you, Jack, that big persimmon was a life saver for me. You see I was given a rubber-tired wheelbarrow and your gift was all I received to eat, therefore, it is all I will have to generate the power to run that wheelbarrow.

Wonder how Methuselah's grand children sized him up. Little three year old Sharon visiting us asked her Grandmother when her Daddy was coming after her. Then she looked up and exclaimed, "Grandmama, I've got a Daddy and you just got an old Granddaddy."

January 31, 1957
Goodlettsville Gazette

Billy the Goat's
Tales of Two Towns

Suppose this week we take an inventory and find out a few facts about television. A few days ago I came up with a startling fact about this new entertainment we enjoy and that is that some of my neighbors and I are responsible for more programs on television than any group of people.

We supply the commercials, and without commercials television would fold up like an unpopular book and stay folded up.

Yes, our products, along with that of a number of other farmers scattered over the country, are advertised over more programs than any other one product in the world.

Furthermore, our products taste good like they should and not only that but the people who use these products "live modern." The only sad note about it is that Miss Agatha has quit appearing on these programs, so since I have realized that I have been contributing to her pleasure all along, it would be nice to see her back again.

Here is the next fact, it is said that some people are born great, some achieve greatness and others have greatness thrust upon them. Well in the first two categories I am a miserable failure, but in the last one I come out with flying colors. I remember building a barn many years ago. It was an enormous structure. One day we reached the place where we had to raise the top rafters over a twenty foot span in the center of the barn to form the comb of the building.

This would have been no great task except for the fact that the farmer having it built had failed to get any long timbers to build a scaffold. The upset of it was he asked me to see if I could not figure some other way to put them up.

That was a long time ago. Surely I must have figured that Darwin was right and relied on inheriting the needed agility from my dim distant ancestors. Anyway, I told him I would try it.

Perched up there on the pinnacle of nothing thirty odd feet in the air with nothing below me but the hard ground, I nailed the rafters together at the top as they were shoved up from either side by my helpers.

Now if you are wondering what this monkey business had to do with television, that old barn later became a theatre and there Dinah Shore made her first appearance and started her brilliant career.

Here is the latest on the subject. We almost had a television casualty out here in the hills the other day. My old friend Bill Breezely had long wanted a television set of his own, so inauguration day he went over to Goodlettsville and bought one and brought it home and set it up to see all the big doings in Washington. However, he had a flat tire before he got home and liked to have missed the whole thing. When he finally got the thing rigged up in the living room at home and turned it on, the President was already on the stage delivering his inaugural address. It was one of those close up pictures with Ike standing there life size looking Bill and his wife right in the face.

Well, things would have worked out fine but for the fact that Mrs. Breezely had made the trip with Bill and had bought herself a suite of long handle underwear because she nearly froze milking the cows this past week of cold weather with the scanty things on she was wearing then. It so happened that when Bill turned the television on she was right in front of it changing to her new underwear. The instant she saw the speaker looking right square at her she screamed and picked up the poker and brained Bill over the head with it, exclaiming, "You lunk head you. What did you turn it on for and me dressing." Then she wailed, "Of all the people in the world to see me stark naked it had to be the President of the United States!"

March 21, 1957
Goodlettsville Gazette

Billy the Goat's
Tales of Two Towns

While mingling with the immense crowds that emerged from Goodlettsville to Shackle Island this past week when two Shackle Island boys returned home, I met up with a number of unexpected people and a very unexpected surprise.

Two strange but charming ladies blocked my pathway, stuck out their hands and said, "Is this Spunk?" I was dumbfounded because I had not been called by that name in over 40 years. I won the nickname at the boarding house in Nashville when I attended school there, because of the way I resisted a fellow student who wouldn't study nor would let me study.

I remember one night I locked myself in my room to study. He kept demanding that I let him in but I refused. So he then took the transom out from over the door and started climbing in. When he became wedged tight in the opening I poured a two-gallon pitcher of water on him, wetting the room below and bringing the landlady up in a hurry. By the way, that landlady is now living is Los Angeles and is 94 years old. Getting back to the ladies, I told them that I once answered to that name. They then asked me if I ever knew Fleece Weighman. Jokingly I answered "'I've been in many a watermelon patch with him."

They then informed me that they were his daughters and by this time there were five of them, all sisters, swarming around me eager to hear what I had to say. You see they all know that their daddy, who has been dead many years, was once a member of the Shackle Island Board of

Health, that band of mischief makers of a half century ago.

They also knew that he was reputed to be the member who signed all correspondence of the Board with that fictitious signature "J. Proctor Knott, Pres." I was reputed to have signed "John Randolph Wilkerson, Secretary and Treasurer." However, this is all supposition.

The one who did the signing was a quiet solemn-faced boy beyond suspicion. Actually, all the victims of the pranks these boys played came to this very fellow to get him to help them find out who did it. This very thing probably was the reason the Board of Health became so famous, or infamous if you like, and their secrets were never found out. Their ringleader, who called all the strikes, posed to the gullible as a secret detective to apprehend them.

Of course, I then told the ladies that I was exaggerating about their father, that I was never in but one melon patch with him and we were invited to that one.

Here is the story: Fleece was about ten years older than the rest of the boys he ran with. He was Sunday School superintendent and also constable in his district. One Sunday morning we were all out in the churchyard, talking when up walked the champion water melon grower in the county. "How is your melon crop?" Fleece asked. "The finest I've ever raised," he answered. "Boys we must go up sometime soon and sample them," continued Fleece, hinting for an invitation for him and the boys.

Believe me, he got it, too. The old gentleman with a twinkle in his eyes said, "Come ahead, boys, anytime you wish; I'll be waiting for you with a loaded shotgun and I'll guarantee everyone of you will get your hides full of shot." "Tell him when we will be there boys," Fleece ordered, and that they did, the night and the hour even to the minute. These boys believed the old bearded gentleman meant exactly what he said. His patch looked like a two–acre nest of large green eggs and he had a tent stretched right in the middle of it from which he guarded it every night.

Well, it has long been a mystery how three stealthy figures crept silently into the back side of the patch, from out of a drain ditch at the appointed time, then walked boldly away across an open field in the bright moonlight a watermelon under each arm and didn't get shot.

Did the owner think they would be dumb enough to come in from the front side and have his eyes riveted in that direction? Or did he think they would not have the audacity to come when they told him they would and consequently stay at the house and sleep that night?

March 28, 1957
Goodlettsville Gazette

**Billy the Goat's
Tales of Two Towns**

While rummaging around the other day, I ran across an old letter written to me a spell ago by my old Uncle Fuller, the only living uncle I have. The old scamp, I firmly believe, will live as long as I do. Perhaps some of you children that read this column would like to read it, especially you that are under forty, so here it is:

Edgefield Junction
Sumner County Route
Date II-XXVII-MCMII

Dear Billy,

I have long had a hankering to write you a letter. Perhaps you and the rest of the boys and girls would like to see all there is to see, so hang out on the front fence all next week if you do.

In case you hear a bugle blowing up the highway around the bend, don't be alarmed. It isn't Gabriel blowing his trumpet, but Jim Garrison, driving two little mules hooked to a covered wagon, calling the women out to sell him chickens, eggs, and butter.

A little later, if you hear a cowbell ringing don't think old Daisy has jumped out of the pasture. That is Taylor Kirkpatrick in another covered wagon calling for his share of country produce.

Then, if you spy a span of small horses hitched to a light spring wagon loaded down with trunks and people, that will be George Giger, driving the Tyree Springs hack, coming from the depot with his first load of summer vacationers.

Hold your breath if you hear a coarse voice calling "haw, Mandy." You will soon see the biggest wagon and the biggest load of lumber you ever laid eyes on and sixteen big mules pulling it. That will be Bill Dorris transporting lumber from E. A. Dorris Milling Company to build Madison Sanitarium.

Then from the other direction perhaps you will see smoke and hear a crunching noise on the highway. This will be a sight no boy will want to miss seeing when that big iron monster slowly approaches pulling a machine as big as a house all painted yellow and striped in green. That will be Bob Bagwell driving a brand new traction engine and pulling a new cyclone thresher to be ready for threshing. As this super attraction rolls up even with you, you will be enthralled, then suddenly your hair will stand straight up on your head and next thing you know you will be back in the house under the bed, but you can come on out again for he won't blow the wild cat any more until he gets to a rail fence where he can pull out some rails to raise more steam.

If you happen to be visiting in the upper end of the county as your often do, hang out on the fence there, too, because you may see the biggest drove of cattle you ever saw coming briskly down the highway seemingly all alone. However, you need not shut the yard gate. They won't run in for there will be a big shepherd dog in the gateway when the cattle get there, while another dog drives them by.

Don't worry, though, about these dogs getting lost when they deliver the cattle to the stockyards. They will go around to the back door of the hotel where they will be well-fed. Then they will trot down to the depot, the conductor of the accommodation will let them up in the caboose and the tired dogs will ride the 20 miles home. Wonder why someone doesn't write a song about these cattle driving dogs, like they did about their owner who answers to the name of the steel driving man in that popular song.

57

Perhaps all of these things above will be relics of the past by the time the century is half gone, but the heroes of the two following relics of bygone days will still be around, I predict, and going strong for many years to come. So, if you are still on the fence and see a fancy harness horse heading you way pulling something noiselessly behind him, that will be Alan Mathis and his best girl in a HMT buggy going over to Uncle Tom Kizer's to see if paw-paws are blooming.

Finally, although you live three miles away, if you hear something coming over Cantrell's Hill that sounds like the devil loose and dragging all his chains, it will be by in about thirty minutes and you will see it is Sam Taylor hi-rollicking along in that chain driven automobile of his scaring the daylights out of all the horses and driving all the mothers frantic trying to keep their kids out of the road.

Signed,
Your Uncle Fuller

This letter was dated fifty odd years ago, so after all it is no April fool.

Billy the Goat's Tales of Two Towns By L. D. R.

I wrote a column on the antics of moonshine drinkers for this week but discarded it, being suddenly convicted that these people are not the greatest menace to life and liberty on our highways.

The killers are the so called respectable people, many of them church goers.

They are drunk on something else.

For like a wagon tire or old casing rolling down a long steep hill they're drunk on speed. The faster they go, the faster they want to go.

Many leave church and drive like the devil was behind them, passing everything on the road to get home in a hurry for no reason whatever.

One has to only drive along and count the rabbits and possums, and the dogs and cats they have ruthlessly killed. Why can't they slow up? God in his wisdom makes all of these animals and they have the right to live the same as the rest of us. If one of these speed demons were to see a small child or an old man, who has reached his second childhood, perhaps they would stop. But if they see a dog in the road they will run over it without trying to avoid it, killing the man or the child by degrees instead of suddenly, as they mourn for their dog.

Two nights ago I went out beside the road and found lifeless the little black Manchester that has been with us a year.

We had kept him for Deba while she was in Germany and all the rest of the time she has been here.

He was just like a child to us and just as smart, so today gloom is spread all over Vertical Plains. Even Harry Truman is sad and looks and listens for the return of his playmate.

I have loved dogs and have been loved by them all my life and am not ashamed of it. So here is a tribute to my little friend that must run before there are any more columns by Billy the Goat. If you don't like the way it is written I didn't expect you to for you don't like dogs and they don't like you.

Goodbye, little doggie, goodbye, we miss you so,
Oh why! Oh why! did you have to go?
When we went to the field you were always there
And you'd bark at anything covered with hair,
But people you loved and trusted them all
And wagged your tail at their friendly call
You were a good little doggie full of fun
And lived and loved and hated none.
May the noble example your life has set
Be a guiding light to all you have met
Dogs have ever been man's best friend
Since the earth was made and time began
If a man has a soul a dog has too
So I made you a coffin, was all I could do.
You were wrapped in your blanket by loving hands
For you were woman's best friend as well as man's.
We laid you to rest where trees abound
That will stop his old car if a demon comes 'round.
The best friend I ever had, little doggie was you
Except big dog Harry who follows me too.
Big dog and I will roam Vertical Plains
While memories of you are all that remains.
So goodbye little doggie at home in the air
You'll be waiting for us sure if we ever get there.
For heaven we are taught is a place of joy
But it would not be, without his dog, to man or boy.

Pray, slow down speeder, and save a dog's life too.

February 5, 1959
Goodlettsville Gazette

Billy the Goat's Tales of Two Towns By L.D.R.

Last year a poll was conducted among the young people of a dozen or more foreign countries as to what they thought of the young people of this country. Every one of them said that the youngsters over here didn't show enough respect for their elders like they did in their respective countries.

Well, maybe we do let them grow up wild like weeds, send them to school and then on to college. Perhaps then some of them do pretend to think we parents are old fogies. Lately I've come to the conclusion that they are one hundred percent right. We are old fogies for sending them to school in the first place, because both the daily paper and TV inform me that the greatest genius this country ever produced never went to school but three months in his whole life.

Thomas A. Edison, no doubt the greatest genius, invented hundreds of useful things for the benefit of mankind and then to amuse us. He presented us with a little contraption that could talk, something only women had ever been able to do before. Thank goodness, though, things haven't always been this way and to prove it I have permission to write a true story about a Shackle Island farmer who minded his father regardless of the consequences.

This man is decidedly the most up to date farmer in that whole community. He has the best kept farm, the best livestock and makes more money than any one else. Singularly there is only one thing that some of you might find fault with him about, though to me it is only a manly virtue.

He chews tobacco.

But why wouldn't he chew the weed, when a single chew of tobacco saved his older brother's life. On the farm where this man grew up they had a big corn crib with sheds built all around it for stock to stand under. An old sow farrowed a litter of pigs under the crib and his older brother crawled under there to count the pigs. The maddened sow lunged at him with angry boos and her mouth open ready to tear him to pieces. He couldn't retreat so he began throwing straw and trash at her but she kept coming. When her mouth was almost at his face he took deadly aim at her and struck her right in the eye with a mouthful of tobacco juice. Squealing in pain she ran back to her pigs.

Once when this farmer was a boy he was carrying his father to catch the train to carry him on to his office in Nashville. The railroad ran in back of the farm and to get to it they had to cross a river that ran through the farm.

His father was dressed in a frock tailed coat and a bee gum hat like gentlemen wore in those days. They were traveling in a one-horse spring wagon and the iron tires which had become loosened in the dry weather were rattling.

When they reached the shallow ford of the river, the father pointed to a deep hole of water up the river and told the boy to drive through it to swell the tires. The boy, who had been in the hole swimming and knew how deep it was, told his father that they couldn't go through there. "Drive through there!" the father commanded, and the boy minded without further argument. Pretty soon the horse was swimming and the water was up to their necks but they made it through alright and the father caught the train.

Maybe you think it was not such a dramatic thing for a man to go to his office wearing wet clothes, and maybe it wasn't, but this man's office was in the State Capitol where he was to meet with dignitaries of that era. For he, himself, was the 25th Governor of Tennessee.★

★(James Price Buchanan, Governor, of Tennessee, 1891–1893)

April 30, 1959
Goodlettsville Gazette

Billy the Goat's Tales of Two Towns By L. D. R.

When Billy the Goat gets pencil cramps and stops writing a clamor starts for the column to continue. Even the women are calling for it, so for their especial benefit here is the story of Susie X that happened many years ago while I was sojourning in a frontier town in the West. It is a secret that has never been told before.

Susie's husband Charlie was the best and most liked fellow in the whole town and Susie was the prettiest woman to look at, but not the best behaved by a long jump. She often had temper tantrums and treated Charlie terribly.

If Charlie spoke to or looked at another woman Susie would slap him and kick him and bawl him out like he was a dog. Then she would likely slap the woman and pull her hair.

Charlie's brother-in-law, Bill, came there from Missouri and went to work in the gypsum mine with him. When Bill learned how Susie was acting, he insisted that the husband take sterner measures with her to curb her tantrums. But Charlie always pleaded that she was only a child and that he loved her too much to get rough with her.

Bill then told the poor fellow that if he would leave and stay gone a few weeks without letting her hear from him that would break her. He then got Supt. Kelly to agree to cooperate with him in a plan he had.

One day Bill came in from the river with the startling news that Charlie had fallen into the swift current and washed away. Search parties claimed they couldn't find hair nor hide of him.

Susie took it pretty hard for awhile. The townspeople didn't know whether it was because her conscience was hurting her for the way she had treated her late husband, or was it because she had no one to bully and boss around.

A short time later a handsome stranger breezed into town. He was supposed to be a mining engineer of some kind. He was medium built and wiry and wore a big western hat fastened on his head by an elastic band under his chin. The first thing the stranger did was visit the widow and sympathize with her. Pretty soon he was going with her regularly and it seemed to be love at first sight.

Susie objected to marrying him so soon, but Supt. Kelly told her she would have to marry at once to hold her house or else move out.

The upset of it was they were married, the Supt. performing the ceremony as he had power to do. After the ceremony, as they were being congratulated, Bill and Supt. Kelly rushed up and kissed the bride, then a rosy cheeked young maiden calmly walked up and kissed the groom.

Well sir, when Susie saw that, she threw one of her tantrums and flew into the girl like a wild cat clawing and scratching her.

Then quicker than a flash the groom had Susie down across his knee spanking her. Just then a cowboy, who seemingly had just happened by for the wedding, stepped up and demanded that he let her alone. "So you want to take her part do you," said the groom as he released Susie. Then before any of us knew what, he yanked the cowboy's pistol out of its holster, tossed it to me and had that cowboy across his knee spanking him so hard you could hear the licks all over town.

Susie stood there looking visibly awed. The groom stepped back to her and told her to go on home and that he was going back to his hotel room and wouldn't come to live with her until she learned to behave herself.

A day or so later Susie saw the groom talking to another girl and accosted her. He gave Susie another good spanking and after that she stayed home and cried all the time, the neighbors said.

Then one morning Mrs. Kelly visited Susie and told her it was a dirty shame the way that new husband had treated her. "No it's not," Susie cried. "I was only getting paid back for the way I always treated poor Charlie."

Taking Susie by the arm, kindly Mrs. Kelly said, "Come on honey let's up and meet the train maybe that will make you feel better."

When they reached the depot, which was also the store and post office where I was a clerk, the whole town had turned out to meet the train and in it came, the whistle wide open like they had the millionaire that owned the road and the town on board.

When the first man stepped off Susie saw it was Charlie X and with a scream she threw her arms around his neck and cried, "Charlie if you will come back to me I'll never boss you anymore." Then she shuddered and said, "But how will I ever get rid of that horrible man. I thought you were dead, Charlie."

Then she felt a soft arm around her shoulder and heard a soft voice say, "You don't have to, little lady, he never existed." When Susie looked up she looked right into the eyes of that new "husband" of hers, but this time he was dressed in women's clothes and had long hair. And to her amazement she heard Charlie exclaim, "What in the world are you doing here, sister, I thought you were back home teaching school."

"Visiting Bill," she answered. Mrs. Kelly at that moment was whispering to Susie to never tell Charlie what had happened and Supt. Kelly had already told the crowd that if anyone ever told him what had happened, he had orders from headquarters to fire him and boot him out of town.

So I am telling this for the first time after nearly fifty years hoping Charlie doesn't read it if he is still living.

July 14, 1960
Goodlettsville Gazette

Billy the Goat's Tales of Two Towns By L. D. R.

The latest pun on this column, Dewey Pickempretty of Shackle Island asking whatever became of the old goat with two tales, well here he is so let's get down to business.

Been asked to solicit contributions for the upkeep of Beech Cemetery. They have been burying people there about 150 years. A Revolutionary War soldier buried there in 1841 (probably has more descendants than any other there except great, great, grandfather of mine) and his grandson buried 50 years later have the tallest grave markers, they are 60 feet high.

Never but once has grave space been refused there, that was when Mrs. Crumbaker's little dog Five Cents, with tiny bells on his collar, ran out in the road and nipped a young mule on the heels. Of course, everyone who has ancestors buried in this cemetery will be glad to contribute or else maybe the World would have been better off had they never had any ancestors. Robert Worsham will take your money, thank you.

William Cuffman, who lives by the pond on Vertical Plains, saw a turtle jump out of the water and grab something. Investigating he found the turtle had bitten a five foot rattlesnake in two and was devouring the monster.

May be absent from writing for awhile; my wife got hold of some money the children gave me Father's Day and had ordered a fifteen dollar pair of shoes for me. Undoubtedly, she must be figuring on taking that long planned trip to the Moon and is taking me with her, because there is no place on Earth I would think of wearing shoes that cost that much.

Probably before you read this the Democrats will have a man nominated for President and he may be a Catholic, but don't let that worry you one bit for there is absolutely no difference in any of the nearly 100 church denominations in the country. They all have the same Bible and worship the same God.

Been reading propaganda put out by one Protestant wing against the Catholics. In answer to such baloney, the Catholics are stronger against Communism than any of the others. In Russia they arrest the priests and put them in prison, while all the churches there that are allowed to hold services are the same Protestant branch as the ones fighting the Catholics here.

Better stop this religious intolerance; it puts you in a bad light. Surely you don't think so much of Krucy you are willing to fight his enemies for him. Let's vote Democratic regardless of who is running—for God in his wisdom created Catholic the same as He did Protestant.

It is nice to be back on my old job, especially since my wages have been increased 200 percent or doubled 20 times since I learned my life-long trade. When I was a boy I picked blackberries for a dime a gallon and sometimes made 60 cents a day. The 4th I picked a gallon and sold them for $2. Saturday I picked three more gallons, now who can beat that for advancement on any job. One lady, however, who has plenty of berries and can't get them picked, has been offered $2.50 a gallon.

Blackberries are the finest ever this year and the most fascinating thing about picking them is listening to the June bugs gripe to the July flies because the white trash are getting all the berries.

Then the old dry fly, as he is called in August, begins singing like a rattlesnake to scare you away. But he can't hold out on the song, there is an intermission and you know it is not a snake.

You laugh up your sleeve when you see an army of chiggers massing to attack because you know they will be repulsed when they discover you ate so much salt you are sweating brine like a pickle.

And there is a small clump of briars with a covey of baby partridges under them. The mother clucks frantically to them as she darts back and forth until she gets them securely hidden, then she flies away.

Such is life on Vertical Plains where the shrill whistle of the bob-white is accompanied by the eerie whistle of the whippoorwill.

September 15, 1960
Goodlettsville Gazette

Billy the Goat's
Tales of Two Towns
By L. D. R.

Last week I received a nice letter from an old schoolmate I hadn't seen or heard from in fifty years. He is W. L. Sprouse of the Veterans Administration in Los Angeles.

Someone had sent him a copy of this paper in which this column ran a story about his uncle, the late R. T. (Pap) Sprouse. So as there is no greater fellow to write about than Pap, we will continue.

He used to tell about the time he was sent to Capses Gap with a four mule log wagon after logs. Arriving at the Gap he found 20 logs, big and little, so he decided he would haul them all in one load. But when he had loaded nineteen of them on the wagon he saw there was no room for the last one.

However, Pap wasn't going to be outdone for he was the champion logger of all time. So, with mules and chains and a lot of know-how, he loaded the remaining log inside the hollow of a big poplar log already on the wagon and brought them to the mill.

Pap was a good friend of mine, who as long as he lived gave me credit for once getting us both out of a very uncomfortable situation.

One day we were both helping two farmers, that lived together, kill hogs. These men were much older and more experienced at the time than I so we made it fine, until we got to the big one. This 500 pound hog we got ready to hang up and Pap and I locked our hands under the monster and packed it to the pole.

But of all things to happen, these two farmers got into a heated argument about which was the best way to raise the hog high enough to put the gambrel stick over the pole, and there we stood in a terrific strain holding the hog while they argued.

Pap was afraid to say anything for fear he would offend the two, but said afterward that they would have stood there and argued until doomsday if I hadn't gotten disgusted and started barking orders to those older men to grab a chain and boom pole and raise the hog up, which they hurriedly obeyed.

The hog was hung in a jiffy and we got relief.

Will Sprouse has forgotten what school we attended together. Well, it was Winthrop out in South Nashville, and I hope he remembers the fight that occurred in the chapel one noon, where the boys assembled to eat their lunch. There were no meals served in schools then.

The fight was between Woodrind and White, two bulldog-built boys, the same size. At that time there was another boy from Goodlettsville going to school there, a gentlemanly fellow so much opposed to rough stuff like fighting that the boys all called him "sister," and he rushed up to stop the fight.

At that moment though, Jim Sands, a big Indian from Oklahoma, much older than the rest of us, locked his arms around the peacemaker and shouted, "Let them fight, boys, I've got sister." And fight they did, too, with fists and chairs until both of them fell out from exhaustion. The incredible thing about it though was that the fight was never reported to the faculty, because had anyone wanted to report it, he wouldn't have dared to rouse the ire of big Jim Sands.

December 22, 1960
Goodlettsville Gazette

Billy the Goat's
Tales of Two Towns
By L.D.R.

Having reached the allotted time of three score and ten a few days ago, just a word about birthday presents. Received the usual array of wearing apparel and a box of cigars from little granddaughter, more cigars than I ever smoked in my whole lifetime.

However, that is not what this story is about. It is about money sent me with instructions to the head comolegers to see that I spent it for clothes, of all things, when I already have plenty and enough for a change any day of the week that I fall in the creek.

Nineteen dollars was the amount, including ten from California and (now this may shock you) five from my little grandson in Goodlettsville. Anyway, he is the only one that will jump up in my lap and kiss me every time he comes to see me. This little fellow has four legs and a tail and his hair is all that's black about him.

Enough money to see the world with so I bought a round trip ticket and rode it out and having already seen the best of the world in half the states, decided to take a look at the worst side of it, so to accomplish this booked passage with Casey Jones.

Further more, our baby daughter had never ridden a train and wanted Daddy to go with her to Lexington to bring back the little grandson who had never ridden one. He was only four, but she was 27.

My, what a surprise! I, who had ridden trains from the Atlantic to the Pacific, sometimes as a paying passenger and sometimes as a hobo, found that she knew more about boarding one than I did.

So, last Tuesday morning Tommy, her husband, took us to the depot and there we waited for the South Wind to arrive from Florida. When it did we rushed out and Deba said "Over this way, Daddy," and I followed her to the steps which I noticed said "hold to banister," but thought nothing of it.

So, like an old fool, I stepped on the thing and the blooming steps were moving. I grabbed the railing and tried to jump backward, but that confounded thing was moving too and down I went expecting all the time to be dragged under the Union Station. However, before the step I was on reached the bottom I jumped and landed out on the runway beside the train.

So, to Louisville we went with tickets as long as our arms. One, the conductor explained, was to ride a Yellow Cab to the Chesapeake and Ohio Station on the bank of the Ohio River. We arrived in Lexington at sundown.

We spent the night with Wallace and Jackie at Shawneetown Apartments at U.K., then overslept an hour and a half, but with Wallace Jr., we managed to get to the station in time.

I'm telling you, when that gold and green painted train rolled in from the mountains right down the main street and the big diesels give a honk or two, it takes a boy a lot older than 70 if his hair don't stand straight up on his head. Then before we could board the thing we had to wait until enough mountaineers piled off to whip the Yankee army had they had guns.

Now for the contrasting sights of our trip: All the way across town we rolled, while traffic was blocked at every street, then past the big distilleries, then through the race horse farms with their white plank fences and horses with heads in the air looking at the train, then past the burley barns, and herds of beef cattle for 20 miles. This, mind you, was on the back side of these farms, but not a buck bush or briar was to be seen as far as the eye could see. The farms were as clean as anyone's parlor, only with giant shade trees that lined the crossroads and dotted the pastures.

Then away down below us we spied a town and started down a deep ravine covered with briars and brambles and gnarled trees, then through a deep tunnel and stopped in the capitol of the state on the banks of the big muddy Kentucky River.

We crossed this river and for miles we traveled up a creek that was frozen over while snow covered the cedars and sycamores that extended as far as we could see.

In a distance of two dozen miles, we had traveled from what world travelers say is the finest country in the world to the roughest, and with a few exceptions it was like that all the way home.

Even as we entered Nashville there were jungles that make it a wonder the wolves and panthers don't catch all the people.

Anyway, Deba and little Wallace enjoyed their first train ride and I got a kick out of my birthday presents from the children.

If any of you have $19.75 given you and want to see this country at its worst then think you have ended up in paradise, just take the L&N to Louisville and then the Chesapeake & Ohio to Lexington and you'll be there plus two whole days on the train, if you come back home on the Pan-American.

January 12, 1961
Goodlettsville Gazette

Billy the Goat's Tales of Two Towns By L. D. R.

The other evening on special invitation I visited the Ladies Debating Club over at Possum Trot. These debates are something new along that line and the ladies are real orators, speaking clear and distinct, never reading their speeches.

After the judges are chosen, a lady is designated to make a speech on any subject she wishes. Then any man in the audience is allowed to take the floor and try to prove that what she said is untrue.

That night a buxom lady that could sling descriptive adjectives like a bulldozer slings mud from a mud hole took the speaker's stand.

Her subject was "Resolved, that people are the most civilized creatures on Earth." She made a lengthy and elaborate talk on the achievements of man and his high state of civilization, then declared that she challenged any man in the house to take the stand and prove otherwise.

Well, sir, you could have heard a pin drop on the floor as the crowd waited for someone to respond. But suddenly they began yelling and clapping their hands as Bill Breezely, an old timer who had made a life-long study of human nature and nature in general, slowly arose and said, "Lady, I accept your challenge."

When Bill reached the stand he studied the judges a moment as if he didn't already know their life's problems and ups and downs. Then he told the audience he was up there to prove to them that dogs are more civilized in the home where civility is an asset to happy living. "Man," he continued, "when he comes home from a hard day's work knows his dog won't growl at him about anything, but the rest of the family he is never sure about."

When he said this, Uncle Si, one of the judges and a well-respected citizen, seemed to get an understanding light in his eye. Of course, Bill knew that the old gentleman's family was always haggling and nagging at him about his old-fashioned ways. "Furthermore," Bill told them, "a dog never worries about money and won't steal like man unless he is hungry."

Hearing this, another judge, Mrs. Getrick, a comely women of 45, appeared to take special interest in what she was hearing. Bill knew he had convinced another judge, because the lady's husband had driven her and her children almost crazy rushing them from before day until after dark in a frantic effort to make a fortune.

"People," the old sage argued, "are often taken in by strangers to their sorrow, but a dog always barks at one. However," he said, "once a dog gets acquainted with a person he will always know him and welcome him with a friendly wag every time he comes around."

This captured the third judge, the old bachelor with the handlebar mustache who often visited his kin and was welcomed only by their dogs since he went broke.

Then to win the audience Bill told them that a dog never spent any time trying to invent some heinous weapon to destroy his enemies, but fought with the weapons nature provided him and could always whip any dog his size or even bigger that attacked him in his own yard.

The buxom lady, in her rejoinder, labeled Bill's arguments preposterous nonsense because "all people," she said, "worshipped some kind of deity." In replying to this Bill admitted that people went to church a couple of hours on Sunday. Then reminded her that dogs had a whole family of gods they worshipped 24 hours a day 7 days a week and had already since the first wild dog took up with the Stone-Age man and adopted him for his god.

Well, I'm sure you all know who won the debate, but here is the last argument my old friend, Bill Breezely, threw in for good measure in his rejoinder, which I know to be true.

Nearly fifty years ago in the Badlands of the Rockies a girl started out in the snow with her faithful dog to visit her grandmother around on the other side of the mesa. On her way she was attacked by five hungry coyotes. Out alone, a dog would take to his heels and run for home, but this dog stayed, braced himself between the vicious brutes, killed three of them and chased the other two away.

February 23, 1961
Goodlettsville Gazette

**Billy the Goat's
Tales of Two Towns
By L. D. R.**

Many times I've been asked for the old Board of Health song describing the activities of a band of mischievous boys that terrorized and tickled Shackle Islanders a half century ago. They began when a prominent chicken breeder placed a little painted house built for something else near the highway to house a pen of chickens. It scared people's horses and the boys were told to move it.

After being threatened with the law for weeks, the boys sent the chicken breeder a nice letter protesting that kind of building so near the road and signed it J. Proctor Knott, Pres. and John Randolph Wilkerson, Sec., Shackle Island Board of Health, Democrat Building, 10th floor Room 6, Shackle Island, Tennessee.

No one ever really got mad and the Board became a legend for their pranks for which they played safe by having as their leader, the Constable, who was single and only a few years older. The song has a moral to it as you will see in the last verse, so here it is:

Verse 1
*Listen all you rounders from far and near,
To story of a gang that roves around here.
Board of Health is their official name,
By moving a hen house they won their fame.
Called to order on Christmas night, in the year of night owls 1908.
The north wind roaring and dark as pitch, they upset that roost and rolled it in a ditch.*
Chorus
Board of Health! They kept out of jail.

Board of Health! Cause their leader was the one put on their trail.
Verse 2
*Pulled up one night in a watermelon patch,
But the news went wild like a war dispatch.
The owner could tell by the hat that was left,
It belonged to a member of the Board of Health.
A man with a shotgun later invited the Board, to visit his patch and risk getting poured.
They set the time, then slipped in behind and for the gunner up front brought back the rinds.*
Verse 3
*Across the bridge and over the hill, pulled up in Long Hollow with an iron will.
The captain says "Boys the thing must not burn.
So all get above her, in the creek she'll turn."
Black Joe, the barber, a member of the Board, along that night laughed long and hard.
"We gonna fix the thing," his laugh began, "So the crazy old coon will never move in."*
Verse 4
*Nothing been doing in some little bit.
When a party at Tobe's that made a great hit.
The night was hot and the ice gave out and the gang got restless and began to stir about.
The captain says "Boys," as they danced a break, "there's one more raid I'd like to make."
"What might that be?" they all asked him.
Sez he, "A raid on that cider of Cousin Jim's."*
Verse 5
*The peanuts brought for tacky party on the hill the hostesses didn't like though the Board paid the bill.
She locked them in the kitchen, with a "dare you to do."
The hulls she found in dresser and feather beds, too.
"Well," says the man in front of the church, "please keep your frogs off my front porch.
And if from my horses I get no report, I'll meet the Board of Health at the next County Court."*
Verse 6
*Everything dull and everything quiet.
Then a dance at Hunt's on a fatal Friday night.*

*The Board got there, but it didn't get back, cause
they went with Daniel whose first name was Jack.
The old lady Gossip, the scandal to recite, was the
    first to learn that the Board got tight.
Hurry, girls, and break all your dates, for you ain't
    gonna go round with such reprobates.*

April 6, 1961
Goodlettsville Gazette

Billy the Goat's
Tales of Two Towns
By L. D. R.

Here is the column again, you have been asking about, with nothing to report except that the paw-paws are in full bloom at Vertical Plains.

Maybe though some of you have wondered what these rough, rugged hills that lie between Goodlettsville and Shackle Island are good for. If you have I'll let you in on a little secret: One of the greatest building programs ever known to man will start soon on these thousands of acres, there will be countless homes built over all the area, some will be permanent homes and many will be summer homes built in the cool shade of many trees. A great increase in population is expected and to meet the need maternity wards will be dispersed everywhere. The homes will be many types and sizes and will not be segregated. The amazing thing about it though is that a lady is sponsoring this gigantic project. She is the richest lady in the world and wields a greater influence than any other. In these hectic days of unemployment there will be an opening for hundreds of guards to patrol these hills armed with rascal beaters to see that nothing hinders, and to top it all off, the pay these guards will receive will make Kennedy's minimum wage proposal and what Hoffa pays his truck drivers look like paupers' pay in comparison.

The only drawback to the project is there will be no construction workers hired, because of the complexity of the way these units are built the lady has her own specially trained builders. Some are already here and others are being flown in daily from the South.

Here now is where you women can get in on this job. All of you living close by will have a chance to take in boarders, for these builders will have to be fed while they are building.

I sure hope my good friends Larry Trabue and Lillard Parks, who sell building materials won't be disappointed too much when I tell them this lady has her own factories and manufactures her own super fine building material.

All of you who are interested in getting a job as a guard and live near Hendersonville contact Lark J. Robbins or Pee Wee Wren. If you are at Goodlettsville call Bob White, or better still drive up to Shackle Island and see Woods and Meadows, real estate brokers who will furnish all the building sites. Of course, all you who haven't caught on you will say that this is a hoax, but it is not.

It is every word the truth for Mother Nature is the lady we refer to and as sure as the sun rises in the East the birds will start building nests soon. Now all of you who have read this are hereby commissioned a guard. Your duty is to fight snakes and predatory animals that might molest the birds and try your best to control all boys with air rifles.

Your pay is the survival of mankind, for without the birds to destroy them we would be plagued with insects and noxious weeds until we couldn't live.

Maybe you think this is a heck of a subject to write about. If you do, you try writing this column next week and we'll print it.

Oh, yes, one fellow in Goodlettsville caught on as soon as he started reading, for during World War II he received a typed letter headed Redd-Bird Construction Co., asking if he would accept the job of supervisor of a major building program near Goodlettsville. This fellow wore out a telephone book and ran the telephone girls in town crazy trying to call this company to accept the job.

But worst of all he showed the letter to a grocer who was so enthused he increased his stock getting ready for the boom and, when he learned later that it was the birds going to start building nests he got so mad he tried to put the FBI on _____ you can guess who.

Anyway, there were no more telephone calls from a fellow that pretended to be from a local union demanding that an old country hunk, with a wife and nine offspring buy snow flake hominy or pay $35 to join the union or quit his job working for the government on Thompson Lane.

April 27, 1961
Goodlettsville Gazette

Billy the Goat's Tales of Two Towns By L. D. R.

Crip Moore surprised me last week when he announced that Mr. and Mrs. L. D. Ralph were celebrating their 44th wedding anniversary, Sunday, April 8th.

It sure didn't seem that long—however, I think I know these two as well as he, so will take up where he left off and give a few odd facts about the hectic harmony of these 44 years.

It took these two more than two years to get started with the product their friends generally associate with them. About this time they moved to Vertical Plains and there they started a seven-year plan, two more years than the Russians ever attempted.

This plan produced six and they had a pretty good start, So they then started a six-year plan which turned out to be a complete failure and the next a three-year plan which yielded 100 percent.—producing three more. In carrying out these plans, she beat him two to one and always saw to it that she got her double portion first, for there were born two girls then a boy, two girls then a boy and two girls and then a boy.

These children so far have gone to school 150 years with two of them still in college, although they are married and have children of their own. This doesn't mean a thing though, for in this country education seldom means you get more pay than hod carrier belonging to some union. It does mean though, that the more learning you have, the farther away from home you have to go to get a job. So these children are scattered all the way from a farmer up in Washington, D. C. to a secretary away down in Columbus, no not Georgia, but Mississippi.

After 44 years living together, and never being away from each other more than two weeks at a time, the only way he can tell she cares a hoot for him is the way she always cautions him to be careful every time he starts out to work in the old Jeep. Why should she worry about that, though, for just the other day a train ran over that Jeep and before he could get it out of the way 50 or 60 automobiles came lumbering over it, too.

The heck of it, he was in it, but they both came out without a scratch. In case you don't believe this just ask Clarence Carr and Harvey Clendening who were sitting on the fence watching.

B-r-r-r, it seems this cold weather is going to spend the summer with us, which reminds us, as every farmer knows, that lambs and pigs seem to always choose the coldest weather of the year to be born in.

Discussing the matter with a prominent sheep man a few days ago, he told me that he had no lambs arrive in the recent zero weather, but said on that very night he had a "Charlie horse: and his mother–in–law had a nightmare

February 1, 1962
Goodlettsville Gazette

Billy the Goat's
Tales of Two Towns
By L. D. R.

Up at Shackle Island last Friday night in Old Beech dining hall we held the third annual Charlie Rice rabbit barbecue. Everything was free.

Charlie furnished thirty-odd rabbits and his wife barbecued them to perfection. We men brought bread, pickles and chips and the ladies brought cakes and pies. All enjoyed the get-together.

About one hundred were present, but thousands in Goodlettsville were represented there, in as much as we were honored by the presence of our banker friends from that town, Marshall Draper, Claude Garrett, and William Martin Ketring.

Charlie Rice is an old time rabbit and coon hunter who holds a record for bagging the game that no one can challenge. Two years ago, getting ready for the first barbecue, he went out with a box of 25 shells and brought in 24 rabbits.

Charlie says his is getting old now and is slipping, but that he is training Norman Frazier, a younger man, to take his place. While Charlie, always in the past in the pursuit of a livelihood, has depended on the fields and the forest, never working in the city, Norman, since he finished school, has commuted to and from town for a living. Charlie went out this time with a box of shells and got only 23 rabbits, missing two. Norman, although there is a difference in his background, came out with exactly the same score. Charlie is a regular attendant of our Men's Bible Class at Old Beech, however, when he was a young man he didn't go to church, but that didn't keep him from teaching a better Sunday School lesson than most of us who have been going to church all our lives.

Nearly fifty years ago he went over across the tracks to another community and hired out to a farmer who was a prominent church man. One day they were plowing corn with double shovels. The farmer was plowing a young mule and as they came around the hill the farmer saw his adjoining neighbor cross over on him and get a drink of water out of his spring. Stopping his mule, the irate farmer told Charlie to hold the young mule for him and told him he had given that fellow two whippings and this time was going to give him a genuine good one.

As the farmer rushed down the hill toward this thirsty neighbor, Charlie called out to him and told him, "If you are so mean that you won't allow your neighbor to get a drink of water, I am quitting right now and if this mule runs away and tears up this field of corn, he can, so far as I care."

Well, the farmer came back and continued plowing, but said nothing. When they went to dinner, Charlie sat down at the table, but his boss sat in the living room with his head bowed over his hands, crying. When they finally got him to talk, he told his folks that for weeks he had been trying to get Charlie to start going to church and that this morning Charlie had taught him more about what Christianity is than all the preachers he had ever come in contact with.

This story has another climax to it though. A few days later Charlie met the neighbor on the highway and told him about the whipping he kept him from getting. The fellow never thanked him, but looked at Charlie and said, "I always thought you was good for something."

March 29, 1962
Goodlettsville Gazette

Billy the Goat's Tales of Two Towns By L. D. R.

All Fools Day, April the first, is just around the corner and will soon be here. People these days don't resort to pranks like they did in days gone by, perhaps it's because they think folks are getting too smart to be fooled . . . . but the smarter they are the harder they fall.

Here is a story of one of the great fools of the past. It is the case of Pud McGruff who all his life had been called Pud. No one knew why, in fact he didn't know himself. Of course, there was a theory that they started calling him pudding when he was a boy and it was whittled down to Pud when he started to school.

SHREWD FELLOW

Pud was a very shrewd fellow who boasted that no one could fool him in any kind of deal. He married and raised a family. When the children grew up they had a telephone installed which Pud took to like a duck to water, calling all the neighbors and having long chats with them. Then came Spring and a new telephone directory, the first one they were listed in. So one day Pud was thumbing through it and found a W. J. McGruff listed in it. He rang the number but got no answer. He hung up and his own phone rang and still no answer when he picked up the receiver and said "Hello." Pud began to grumble and his wife asked what was the matter. He explained to her and she, with a twinkle in her eye, told him to wait until after supper and call again, maybe they would be home.

After supper Pud rushed out in the hall and dialed the number again and his wife, over the extension in the kitchen answered hello in a honeyed voice. Pud told her who he was and asked who it was speaking.

She told him she was Mrs. W. J. McGruff, that her husband was busy at the moment and that she would be glad to talk to him. Pud told her he thought he might rake up kin with them and asked where W. J. was born. She, of course, named the upper country where Pud came from and he got excited.

She then told him she had heard her husband's parents had twin boys and because two were more than they bargained for they gave one away to an uncle and aunt and that, possibly, he and W. J. were twin brothers.

TOO TIGHT

Then she wound up the conversation by telling him she would invite them over for supper some evening, but that W. J. was too tight to buy anything for her to cook, so if he would have his wife prepare a nice supper they would come over and eat with them Saturday evening and specified a pot of beans and a blackberry pie with plenty of pork barbecue to go with it.

Pud called his wife from the kitchen and told her of the plan and asked if she had any canned berries and beans. She told him she had plenty, but that they would probably want store bought beans. The upset of it all was Pud bought ten pounds of navy beans (the first he had bought) and a pork shoulder.

A great feast was prepared that night, and while Pud was much disturbed about the twin that was given away because he was an only child, he could hardly wait for the company to arrive.

One of his grown daughters was the one that finally got him to come to the table, when she convinced him that he, himself, was W. J. McGruff according to old records, and that it was her mama he was talking to all the time from the extension in the kitchen. "Why did you fool him, Mama?" one of the little ones asked.

"Because it was the first day of April" she answered. "Besides he fooled me last year when he told me he was getting me something special for our wedding anniversary." "Well, didn't he?" another piped in. "Sure he did," she admitted. "He got me a $1.25 broom on special for 98 cents."

August 9, 1962
Goodlettsville Gazette

Billy the Goat's
Tales of Two Towns
By L. D. R.

Visited Leon McCreary at his place of business in White House yesterday afternoon. Have known him a long time but just learned on this visit that his given name is Leon. So now I no longer wonder why he is such a jolly good fellow. Spell it backwards and it means Christmas.

Anyway, he asked if the grandchildren were still with us, then demanded that I write this column saying he was a subscriber expecting to read it. However, I didn't tell him that I was on my way to Clearview to visit my grandson's wild watermelon patch. Yes, they were wild, they had never been planted. At the back door beside the patio, the vines came up voluntarily and on a space 10 feet square there are 20 melons the size we see in the stores. They were all covered over with Bermuda grass. The secret is they were kept watered daily.

Working this summer on Vertical Plains with briar blade, hoe, and turning cider mill, I've often wished I could take a good long rest. Well, I took it election day. 12 long hours sitting in a straight chair or sauntering around helping hold election at Madison Creek and when night came I was more tired than I ever was in my whole life.

AGAINST TWO

I was not for either of the three candidates for governor but I did vote against two of them because all they did was ride the third one, bug hunting because he went frog hunting with Billie Sol a time or two. Consequently, I didn't lose my vote for governor for the first time in many moons.

One of the lady judges that day said it would be a blessing if the man from Lookout Mountain town got beat, because it would save future school children in history student the arduous task of learning to pronounce his name, "O Jetty." This man, it seems, is the first one to run for that office from that neck of the woods since James B. Frazier was governor. That gentleman became the most unpopular governor Tennessee ever had with voters around Shackle Island when he appointed himself U. S. Senator to fill the place of the late William B. Bate of Sumner County.

That was 55 or more years ago and maybe you wonder how I remember it so well, so here is the reason. I was going to school at old St. Francis schoolhouse at Shackle Island. One day they were having a class in Tennessee history. The lesson was about John Sevier, the first governor of Tennessee. There was a large boy in this class with the same name of the governor. This boy was tops on the playground and could knock a ball further than any of us, but he wouldn't study and, of course, never knew his lesson.

Professor Tom Hunter, knowing the boy's weakness, thought he would give him an easy question he could answer, so he said to him, "Name a great man in this period of history." The boy looked confused and began shuffling on his seat but it so happened that an older boy doing a problem on the blackboard whispered something to the confused boy that the teacher and all 76 students in the one room school didn't hear or know about. Then the boy's face, that was asked the question, brightened up and he blatted out so all of us could hear, "Governor Frazier was a great man." Everybody there knew his answer should have been John Sevier and also knew how unpopular Frazier was, so the roar of laughter it provoked was deafening and long lasting. The teacher joined us and let us laugh as long as we wanted to.

December 6, 1962
Goodlettsville Gazette

Billy the Goat's
Tales of Two Towns
By L. D. R.

I wonder sometimes why I write this column. I get my pay just the same, for the editor gives a dam or two each week, whether I write it or not. Beg your pardon, I'm not using profanity, for a dam means two cents in Chinese money, which is about what it costs to mail the paper to me.

Pondering about what to write, I dreamed I was writing a society column and here is what I wrote: You will find a conglomeration of most of the human ills known to man, see how many you can recognize.

This event was an all-day party. The first guest to arrive was Miss Afe Eve Evryautumn, along with Miss Fay Tigue, who was escorted by the Ness twins, Try Edd Ness and Lay Z Ness.

Another guest was Coll Ick, who was afraid to eat most all they put on his plate, but thoughtfully wrapped it up to carry it home to his dog. Also present was Coll's old-maid aunt Tiz. A well-dressed man who was there passing out seed catalogues approached the old lady and said, "Miss Ick, I am Burpee." To this she answered, "Land sakes man, don't talk. I get that way myself sometimes." An old hound followed one fellow there, and slipped in the house and started crawling under the bed. When his master saw the dog, he yelled, "Get out of here, you son of a tinker!" He could have called the critter like Harry Truman called Drew Pearson and been more correct.

Rhew Johnson, like he always does, brought his mattock with him, or grubbing hoe we call it. Because he makes his living digging ginseng in summer and sarsaparilla in the winter, they all dubbed him Rheumatic.

One guest didn't stay but a short time. He was on his way to Hot Springs and when he left several called after him and said "Authar, write us."

A very beautiful girl was there, but she couldn't talk above a whisper. Her name was Laureen Ghitus.

Then a beggar came by while dinner was being served and asked for a handout. They called him Lum. Putting two and two together, he was evidently Lumbeggar.

This party was held at a farm house. That afternoon some of the children were sent out to gather up the eggs, and were told if any of the hens were setting to get the eggs from under them, too. Well, they seemingly had all their hens named, for soon the children came back crying, "Angina pecked us."

There was one bearded Communist present, whose name was Svenscratchski. (Translate it, if you can. It sounds like something you could only have three times before you become old enough to vote.)

Bright Breezely was there all dolled out, ready to set in a plush bottomed rocking chair like he does at home. But, at the party he had to sit on a nail keg, which was plainly a case of Bright's disease.

The people at this gathering had lengthy discussion of world affairs, especially India Jestion, all caused by an overdose of Chinamen. The only time they touched on religious matters was their talk about infidels or bombers and missiles in Fidel's Cuba.

Oh yes, there was one fellow there who seemed to be better acquainted with the folks than any of the others and they seemed to know him better, too. They called him Bad. He spied me, a stranger, and shook my hand and told me he was Bad Cole, and that he had corns on both his feet caused by reading my corny columns in the paper. I told him I had them on both my feet, too, from writing the columns, but that this was the first time since I'd been writing I had ever contracted a bad cold.

Probably there were others I've failed to mention, but what struck me, or failed to strike me I am thankful, was the absence of the most dreadful of all the diseases of mankind. There was a good reason they were absent, for only a pig path led to this place and they couldn't get there. All who came had to walk, so I'm leaving you to guess what this dreadful menace to mankind is.

January 17, 1963
Goodlettsville Gazette

Billy the Goat's Tales of Two Towns By L. D. R.

When I complained to the man who edits this column about not knowing anything to write, he suggested that I write about past experiences, seemingly aware that all my life I've been a jack-of-all-trades and apparently good at none or else I would now be a millionaire.

So here goes to let you know that Billy the Goat has held his own for the past 40 years. At that time I was hauling shade trees to Goodlettsville and setting them out for customers. Yesterday I went "way down yonder in the paw-paw patch" and dug a fine Tennessee banana tree and carried it over to the banker at Goodlettsville.

Now I'd like to say this, if any of you want any shade trees set out give a ring at UL 9-2667. If the editor wants to promote shade in the Summer time and beans and chunk meat at Vertical Plains in the Winter, he'll run this in the For Sale Column for me.

While setting out shade trees in February 40 years ago, I took laryngitis and couldn't talk, but I knew that Uncle Will, my old bachelor uncle, had a full quart of moonshine he had never touched and I also knew why. So I stopped by one morning and told him the best I could whisper that I wanted a shot of it to clear up my throat.

"I grannies alive," he yelled, "that stuff will kill you.!"

But I insisted, and he poured me a glass half full of the poison figuring, I am sure, on making a guinea pig out of me—if it didn't kill me, then he would try it himself.

I knew why he thought it would kill me. He had given the fellow who he had sent after it a little swig, and he got as drunk as a bald owl and as sick as a horse. But what Uncle Will didn't know and I did was that this fellow had bought himself a full quart and had drunk every drop of it before he took that little swig Uncle Will gave him.

Well, I gulped the stuff down, and lit out for home, because it flew to my head immediately. Then, to cap the stack, Uncle Will jumped up to go home with me. Luckily, he never knew how near that drink came to killing him. That old T Model was the first ever to do the "Twist" as it came down Long Hollow Pike. He thought, of course, that I was just dodging the ruts in the road.

However, now, if any of you want any shade trees, don't worry about me taking laryngitis. I have a quart of wine as strong as Uncle Will's moonshine, which was given me by a state geologist for the privilege of geologizing Vertical Plains anytime he wishes.

Here is some news that might be of interest:

Harry Truman and Jack Kennedy, my two dogs, went coon hunting the other Saturday night. They treed and barked for an hour like they were ready to eat something up before I got out of bed and went to see about them. That was at 12, midnight.

When I got to them, Harry was there on one side of the garden fence, barking for all he was worth, and I thought Jack was on the other side. As I looked up into the tree, with only starlight to see by, I saw a big wooly monster up there, three or four feet long and as big around as a backlog. I started to run back to the house to get my gun, thinking it was a wildcat, but about that time it fell out. And I saw it was Jack Kennedy! About six inches above where he had been was a big coon. I made it jump out, and the dogs grabbed it.

Knowing you are going to say this is a lie, let me explain: There was a shock of corn around this tree, which enabled the dog to reach the first limb.

February 28, 1963
Goodlettsville Gazette

Billy the Goat's
Tales of Two Towns
By L. D. R.

Reading the papers it seems that something new is sweeping the country in the shape of a walking marathon Since this thing started at the suggestion of officials in Washington, I believe they have something going that will be of a great service to the whole country. They can easily accomplish something now that they have been trying to do for years, but failed. They can get rid of all the surplus grain the government has stored up.

These long walks are going to create stronger appetites, which in turn will call for eating more bread, which, as you know, is made from grain and has always been considered the "staff of life." From the beginning up to four or five decades ago, grain was the fuel used to create horse power, for people to take trips to remote places on stage coaches and wagon trains. Also, it was used to create the power for pulling farm machinery.

So, if this exercise will induce nearly 50 million people in this country to eat two loaves of bread a day, instead of only one, in a year's time it would amount to 365 million bushels of wheat now in storage bins.

Some people are afraid to eat bread because they have been told it is fattening, but bread or grain won't even fatten a hog if he has walked several miles between feedings.

Others don't eat bread because they prefer to spend their money on something else. For instance an old uncle of mine, who was thin and gaunt but also a hearty eater, told me this story: He was working with a bunch of boys when one day they gave one of the men $20 and sent him to the nearest town, 50 miles

away, to buy a week's supply of bread and whiskey. The cowboy brought back a dollar's worth of bread and nineteen dollar's worth of whiskey. The rest of the cowboys came near to mobbing him when he returned because he had spent so much for bread. In fact, they had already grabbed him and were taking him to the water trough to throw him in when my uncle stopped them. He told them the bread only amounted to 20 loaves and he could eat that much himself in a week's time and lack one loaf having enough. Furthermore, he told them they could drink their 9 ½ gallons of whiskey, and he would eat the bread.

About 60 years ago in Shackle Island, a man named Montgomery Jefferson went west and stayed a few years. When he came back he told me a story that was in contrast to this, pointing out how people once ate bread Every Summer, he said, while in California he worked as a cook on a combine. His speaking of combines back then, incidentally, amazed me, for there were no combines in Tennessee. Farmers cut their wheat with binders and afterwards a thresher pulled into the field and threshed it, dotting the countryside everywhere with huge straw stacks, around which the best watermelons grew.

But back to my story: Jeff said that where he worked they had one whole county in wheat, all in one field. On the big combines, pulled by a giant tractor engine, they had a mill grinding the wheat into flour. They had cooking equipment in the fields with the crews, and Jeff cooked biscuits out of the flour ground right there in the field four times per day. The night crew had to eat at midnight, incidentally.

As far as eating the surplus grain is concerned, I am ready to help, but I prefer the greater portion of my grain in the form of dough wrapped around sugar and fruit or berries and baked into an old-fashioned cobbler pie. No matter what sized pan—the bigger, the better.

October 3, 1963
Goodlettsville Gazette

Billy the Goat's Tales of Two Towns By L. D. R.

A few days ago I received a telegram from California telling me that a very dear friend of ours had died there at the age of 95—Cousin Mina Kirkpatrick.

In spite of the fact that she once gave me the most awful bawling out I ever received, she was one of the most amiable and gracious ladies I ever knew During the several years I went to school and later worked in Nashville she was my landlady.

She ran a boarding house on Eighth Avenue, near the Custom House. A fellow student there would neither study nor let me study, because he wanted to frolic all the time. On account of this, Cousin Mina moved me to an adjoining room away from him. Immediately, he came to my room and demanded that I let him in. I refused.

Then he went to his room, climbed upon the bed, took out the transom and started to crawl through the opening over the door. A large pitcher of water was on my dresser. I grabbed it and began pouring it on him. This only made him more determined to get in, and he made another surge forward, and got stuck in the transom.

As the water began pouring through downstairs, up came Cousin Mina. There I stood with the pitcher in my hand and him hung in the transom. Well, sir, she really got us told until he finally squirmed loose and fell back into his own room.

Later, I walked with her to the city market for provisions, and she laughed all the way about the rowdy boy getting hung in the transom and the wetting I gave him with the pitcher of water.

One Sunday afternoon I remember a novelty salesman from New York came and rented a room for a week. On Wednesday he found himself alone in the parlor and he burned his full name on the white enamel hearth with a red hot poker. Cousin Mina was furious, but she wouldn't make him leave since he had paid his rent for a week.

This, mind you, was years before World War I and decades before Hitler in World War II started his crusade to rid Germany of the Jews. However, we school boys, with Cousin Mina's permission, hit on a plan, such as Hitler never even thought of, to rid the boarding house of its unwelcome guest.

That night he came in at midnight caterwauling like a wild cat, as he had the previous nights, and went into his room. We already had fastened a black sewing thread to the headboard of his old wooden bed, and had pulled it through the transom and down the hall to our room where the lights were all out.

The first time we sawed down on that thread with a large piece of rosin, his feet hit the floor, and his light came on. Evidently, he saw there was nothing in the room and went back to bed.

We then rubbed the thread furiously, and he jumped out of bed again. This time he came out in the hall and looked in the bathroom, then came to our room and tried to force his way in. We had the door locked and all our shoulders against it.

The third time his light went out we waited a few minutes, then gave the thread and rosin "Hail Columbia." Down the stairs he crept, as quiet as a mouse with all his belongings, and that was the last we ever heard of Max. He left only his name emblazoned on the hearth for us to remember him by.

Cousin Ed Lanier and wife Fanny May visited Vertical Plains this week. Cousin Ed is a very interesting conversationalist. While a young man he worked as a merchant and traveled over most every state in the Union installing shoe making machines and repairing them when they broke down.

He usually tells something that makes a good story, but this time he only told about passing through a town that had the same name as his. I can't believe he told all there is to this story, because I recall one similar that had more to it.

Here is the story: A man named Lanier was traveling on a train. In the smoker he found a pocket book containing four one dollar bills and a quarter. He put his find into his pocket and returned to his seat. The train sped on. No one mentioned losing any money. Soon it stopped in a little town and the porter walked in and yelled, "Lanier."

The fellow named Lanier jumped up and asked what was the matter. The porter said, "The train has stopped, waiting for 425."

"Well, here it is," declared Lanier, as he handed him the money.

The porter thanked the fellow and pocketed the money.

Then as Lanier set back down a fast banana train came thundering by, and on the engine the fellow read "No. 425." As his train rolled by the depot, he read "Lanier, GA," and then he realized he had been hornswoggled.

So you can't blame a fellow for not telling the last part of this story.

April 9, 1964
Goodlettsville Gazette

Billy the Goat's Tales of Two Towns By L. D. R.

Continuing the story about the Shackle Island gang of boys who acquired the high sounding name of the Board of Health:

Back then, more than a half century ago, there were no radios, televisions, or even a picture show where these boys could go for amusement. There was only one automobile in the whole district in which they could hitch a ride. It was chain driven and made as much noise as a half dozen chain saws. This being the case, the boys spent a lot of their time possum hunting to while away the long winter nights, but the demons of devilment most always saw to it that they got into mischief before they returned back home.

One night a half dozen of them were out hunting in the Bony Pig neighborhood when they crossed over a fence into a big apple orchard, hoping to find an apple or two still on the trees, but no luck. They found the orchard had been planted in sorghum that year. It had already been harvested and made into molasses.

However, on the roots of the sorghum there was a mass of frost-bitten suckers which everyone knew were fatal to cows should they eat them. This orchard belonged to a peddler who made a living partially by driving a covered wagon around over the country. He'd stop at farm houses and blow a bugle, and in this manner he let farm women know he had arrived so they would trade their chickens and eggs and butter with him, which he took to Nashville once a week to feed the population there.

When the boys left the orchard they came out the front way, where instead of a gate, three wide planks were propped up to a stop gap. As the last boy crawled through, the planks all came tumbling down, making a loud noise. This happened right in front of the peddler's house, and the lights were still on. The boys darted out into the thick weeds and hid, and out came the peddler. He had a lantern in his hand, and was muttering something about the old cow in the sorghum patch.

He went all over the patch shouting, "Ho-o-ey!" And he was getting madder every step. Finally he came out and propped the planks back up across the gap.

As soon as he went back into the house the planks were torn down again, and out again came the irate peddler. Once more he combed the orchard for the cow, then put the planks back into place and went to the house. However, this time as he entered, he yelled, "All right, old fellow, I'll be ready for you next time."

The boys saw him through the window. He picked up his shotgun and started out the back door, and then the boys took to their heels, for they knew none of them were immune to shotgun pellets. Besides, they thought the fun was over, but it had only begun.

Out on the public road a half mile away, as the boys topped a hill, they heard the clop, clop of a mule's hooves, and they knew it was the peddler's big brawny son riding that mule. To keep from being recognized they lay down in a narrow strip of broom sage between the road and the fence.

Things would have been all right, but when that cranky mule got almost to the broom sage he gave a loud snort and lunged backwards down hill. The boy kept urging the mule forward, and then apparently he suspected someone in the sage.

He yelled, "You make this mule throw me and there'll be more h——l raised around here than ever before."

After that the sage was shaken a little each time the mule approached, and his rider never did get him by. But he did manage to get him on the bank on the far side of the creek and rode by cussing like a sailor until one of the boys fired a .22 rifle in the air. Then he hushed and headed for home.

Here is another story that only involves two of the boys:

Back then squirrel hunters reported seeing a big gray wolf in the wooded hills of Long Hollow. These two were going around a high ridge hunting one night when they heard loud voices and saw two lanterns down in a deep hollow below them. The boys listened and then discovered it was an elderly white man and an elderly Negro whom they knew well.

One of the boys let out an unearthly squall like a wild cat, and then ran around the hill in the dry leaves and brush.

"Listen—that's that damn wolf," the Negro said.

Almost at once they raised their shotguns and emptied both barrels, spent shot falling in the leaves all around the boy.

That was just what the boy wanted, for he knew it would take them ten minutes or more to reload their old muzzle loaders, so he headed straight towards them with more wild cat screams. Their four dogs were scared so badly they headed for home, yelping and barking. Behind the dogs went their masters.

The men hollered, "Here! Here!" But in vain they tried to get the dogs to come back for them. Several times they fired caps on their old guns, but they never stopped to ram powder and shot down the barrels.

Don't say they wouldn't, for I tried it and I know.

April 29, 1965
Gazette & Star News

Billy the Goat's
Tales of Two Towns
By L. D. R.

Such weather! Spring is so late that polk sallet has just begun to grow. Some people call it "poke sallet" incidentally.

Reminds me of the hot presidential race which occurred over a hundred years ago, which I remember hearing my Grandma tell about. At that time James K. Polk of Tennessee ran against Henry Clay of Kentucky. She stated that many Polk supporters carried a big "polk" stalk, laden with berries, in their buggies and wagons as they traveled about the country. They also, she said, displayed signs on their vehicles which read:

> *"Henry Clay and Frelinghysen,*
> *Nothing but a dose of pisen."*

Likewise, Clay supporters, with the wheels of their vehicles bedecked with red clay, had signs reading:

> *"James K. Polk and George*
> *McDallas*
> *One for the devil, the other for the gallows."*

However, what I started to say is that Goodlettsville is one place where "polk" grows and thrives the year 'round. I saw John Ed Polk there April Fool's Day, and he told me while he was vacationing in Florida he read this column, and enjoyed it. Thank you, John Ed. But such a name! Just try saying it over and over and it will sound like you're saying "John et polk," making you wonder if my esteemed friend, John Ed, has been eating "polk" sallet for a Spring tonic.

Another interesting thing about this town is the strange coincidence of the town's two leading citizens having almost identical twin names, although they are no kin whatever, and come from different necks of the woods. Their first names, a name few people have, is exactly the same and their last names are the same except for the "ett" and the "ison." One of them manages the town, the other the "dough" that keeps the town alive. Still more coincidences, they belong to the same church, both have one son and one daughter each. And to cap it off, the sons have the same names as the two most prolific writers in the New Testament. And if you know the names of the two most important mothers in the beginning of the New Testament, you know the daughters' names.

Maybe it might interest you to know the biggest loan ever made by the Goodlettsville Bank was made to Hollywood when the name of its oldest director, Mr. Charlie Cartwright, who is up in his 90's, was loaned to use in "Bonanza."

Here is a personal problem of mine: Two brothers own a fine stock farm at the north edge of town. One brother is a doctor, the other is a farmer. A short time ago we bought a yearling Angus bull from the brothers, and my problem is whether to name the bull Bennett Thomas or Thomas Bennett. If you care to know the last name of the brothers, take the first syllable in the name of a fierce Arctic bear and add to it the last syllable in the name of a rooster's craw—and you have it.

Nearly a half century ago the writer of this column took some very conspicuous advice, but strange as it may sound, he took the advice many, many years before it was given or even thought of. The advice was "Stop and Go with Hester." So I have been following her around ever since like a faithful old dog.

Thursday, April 8, our obliging daughter, Mrs. Bradley, carried her mother and me out to supper, it being the occasion of our 48th wedding anniversary. That was one time I learned a very important lesson, namely, it never pays to let anyone be too nice to you.

We ate at a restaurant just over the line in Kentucky, and I ordered a hamburger, as I usually do, but Mrs. Bradley insisted that I order a Salisbury steak with gravy and vegetables instead. I, fool like, agreed, but of all things, they brought me cornbread to eat with it! Henceforth, I'll stick to hamburgers, as long as they don't serve them with cornbread. That is one thing I always thought women baked to crumble up to feed to baby chickens.

A word now about our courtship: She was a country girl, and I was just as country as any rube you ever saw, so I courted her in words she could understand. Like, for instance, "My love for thee will ever flow. Like 'lasses down a "tater row."

I hereby declare it still flows just the same, and she still thinks a lot of me, but she won't admit it to anyone, not even to me. However, when I start out in the Jeep, she always cautions me to "drive carefully." Then if I tell her she doesn't think much of me, she always answers, "I know I don't—just don't want the Jeep torn up."

She lets the secret out, though, every time she sends me on an errand on foot across the busy street in Goodlettsville. It's always, "Be careful and watch out for cars."

November 3, 1965
Gazette & Star News

Billy the Goat's
Tales of Two Towns
By L. D. R.

I trust it won't be amiss to write a social column at this time about the Fall Festival sponsored by the greatest lady in the world. Of course, all of you know who she is. This was held over on Tywhoppity, a round hill covered with trees back in the forest.

It began at daybreak one morning with Bob White whistling, "Peas ripe—not quite," while Morna Dove cooed all around him.

Red Fox was scheduled to be the barker in calling out the acts, but when Red barked the first time old Leed Hound on a cold trail heard him, and here he came. These two Played "Comin' Round the Mountain," with Red in front and Leed right behind until both became exhausted and had to lie down and relax.

Caw Crow and his clan did the cheering, and they were heard for miles around. Tarzan Squirrel and a host of his trapeze artists entertained by doing great acrobatic feats on the limbs of the trees overhead.

As for the eats, this generous old lady provided oodles of nuts, acorns, beech mast, fox grapes, and persimmons, and for those who didn't eat such goodies there was plenty of green grass and wild lettuce.

Rac Coon was there boasting he could whip anything that showed up. Pretty soon a big old sow with 10 pigs came along rooting in the leaves for mast. It seemed for a moment she would break up the festival.

Rac tried to run her away, but she lunged at him with her mouth wide open and he made a hasty retreat, resulting in all of them giving him the horse laugh. Rac was cunning,

though. He maneuvered around her a bit then jumped upon her back, seized her stumpy tail with his sharp teeth and began scratching her with his long claws—and she was long gone.

Old Hen Hawk was there with a lame wing, and couldn't take part in the activities, but Darter Hawk did a spectacular dive from high up in the air. Having no water to dive into, she intended to land on Peter Rabbit's back. But Peter was too quick for her. He kept his back behind him and grabbed Darter and hugged and kissed her, which gave them all another horse laugh.

Only once was the festival interrupted by a commercial. That was when Tennessee Pride put on a live sausage advertisement with the appearance of A. Groundhog on the scene.

When it came time for music, they had it. Mr. and Mrs. Gaye Mockingbird rendered a duet, "Mockingbird on the Hill." Crested Logcock simulated the drums by pecking on an old dead tree. Jenny Wren and a lot of other small birds came flitting around and chirping, while a large flock of wild geese in V formation flew over with their familiar honk.

Sammy Possum gripped the loose end of a long grape vine with the end of his tail and swung around and around to show them all how the astronauts circled the earth. Old Tom Kaat (no kin to Jim Kaat, the World series pitcher) saw all these small fry birds and small animals so congenially assembled together, and started creeping slyly in to make a catch. Fortunately, there was another cat present, this one no kin either to Mud Cat, the other Twins pitcher. So policeman Pole Cat spied old Tom and saw what he was up to, then quickly shot the old rascal in the eye with tear gas. The last we heard from Old Tom he was moving on across the hills.

The most valuable thing at the festival was a mink stole, and the most outrageous thing to happen occurred when old Miss Mink stole an egg out of Mr. and Mrs. Robin's nest while they robbed old Leed Hound of all the fleas on him as he lay sleeping.

Late visitors arrived by air, dressed in gaudy blue uniforms. They had flown from Jay Bird's Landing, and all started, "Half, half," as soon as they arrived, just like they do when you find them in your apple orchard after they have eaten up half the apples and are yelling for the other half.

All this noise woke up old Leed Hound. He saw Peter Rabbit running away in a terrible hurry, and noticed that all the guests, with the exception of a few of the larger ones, were up in the trees very excited. Looking around Leed saw that Willie Wesel, the smallest and most ferocious denizen of the forest had ventured on the scene. Willie had been known to kill every chicken on the roost just for their blood. Leed hesitated a moment until he heard a plaintive voice deep in the wilderness, crying "Whip-poor-will," then with a yelp and a bound he was after Willie, chased him to his den beyond Snipe Hunt Ravine, then trotted off home.

Red Fox, master of ceremonies, said it was time to adjourn, and asked who would clean up the grounds, but no one answered. Then old Jude Owl called out angrily from a tall tree, "Who-o, who-o?" as if he wanted a volunteer.

Just then an ancient apparition with wings spread wide circled low over the treetops, and the wise old judge called out again, "Who-o, who-o?" Twas a happy ending for the festival, because the participants knew that Mother Nature had dispatched Old Buzz and his scavenger force to do the job for them.

Thanks to Old Leed and Officer Cat—there were no casualties, so Buzz's job was light.

Some will say not a word of this is true, but prove it isn't if you can.

December 9, 1965
Gazette & Star News

Billy the Goat's Tales of Two Towns By L. D. R.

Shackle Island is in the 7th District of Sumner County. People around there have always been law-abiding and clever—and still are. Up in the hills above there have lived some very clever people in the past—as to their being law-abiding, you can be the judge:

One was a farmer who most of his life raised vegetables which he hauled to the Nashville market. When horse and wagons went out of style he got himself an old beat-up truck to haul in, and he was a careful driver.

One day when he started home, out North First Street, a traffic cop stopped him and gave him a ticket for driving too slow. The next time the farmer started home, he saw this cop and stopped and told him that because he had been fined $10 for diving too slow, he was going to give the cop a chance to fine him for speeding, if the cop could catch him. So he stepped on the gas, and lit out for home. The cop pulled out behind him. When the cop roared into Goodlettsville with the siren wide open he saw the old beat-up truck going over the hill out of town. The same thing happened when the cop sped through Millersville. He saw the truck ready to climb the ridge, and when he reached the top of that long hill, he got a glimpse of the truck turning into a side road. He followed until he saw the truck parked at the farmer's home. So he drove up in front of the house, stopped his car, then got out, tipped his hat, got back in his car and drove away. Thanks to Mrs. Hester for telling me this one a short time ago.

These people who live in the hills are not only clever, but they have compassion. Back during the depression some of them took pity on the fellows in the penitentiary who work so hard making auto license plates, so they made their own license plates. Maybe they would be still making them today if one fellow hadn't got in a hurry and made such a poor job he got caught.

There was Cousin Bob—he grew up in these very hills. One day a tight-wad farmer told him and another boy to bring a couple of fat hens to his house on a certain night and they would have chicken supper. Cousin Bob told the fellow that he didn't have any fat hens to bring. "Just get out and steal two," he told the boys, and they said they would.

On the appointed night just after good dark, the boys appeared at the farmer's kitchen door with two fat domineckers—the kind that most everyone raised back then. The hens were dressed and cooked into chicken and dumplings, and all present at the supper had a very enjoyable meal. The farmer complimented the boys for being such good judges of fat hens, then he asked if they would mind telling him where they got the hens.

"Not a bit in the world," Cousin Bob said. "We got them off your chicken roost just before we came to the kitchen door."

In these same hills a native used to make moonshine. It must have been pretty good stuff. An old bachelor uncle of mine sent a fellow there to get him a quart for medicine. I asked him to give me a drink for laryngitis, and he answered, "Gracious alive! That stuff will kill you."

I told him not to worry about that, because I would soon starve to death anyway, since I couldn't talk loud enough to ask for something to eat.

He poured me out a big shot, which I drank, then started to get in my car. He said he was going home with me, but he never knew how near he came to getting killed, riding that mile down the pike with a drunken driver. It was the only time I ever tasted moonshine, and the only time I was ever drunk, but a fellow doesn't have to stay drunk. I grabbed a grubbing hoe and started digging up an onion bed. In 15 minutes I was sober and my laryngitis was completely cured. I could have yelled loud enough to have heard my echo from the moon.

My advice: If you drink, leave your car and walk home, then walk back and get it, and you'll be sober enough to drive without endangering the lives of others.

By the way, the reason Uncle Will thought moonshine would kill me was because he gave the fellow he sent after it a little shot, and he became awfully sick. What he didn't know was that fellow had already drunk a whole quart he had bought for himself.

Now if you are not convinced these hill people of the past were clever, here is one that will convince you. This happened nearly a century ago:

Sheriff Tobe Dodd had a warrant for one of these men for stealing a horse. He found the man out at work near his house, and told him he would have to carry him to jail. The man asked the sheriff to allow him to go in the house and change his shoes. The sheriff agreed, and stood out in the yard waiting for him. The man changed his shoes, but that's not all. He changed to his wife's shoes—also her stockings, her dress and sun bonnet, then picked up the milk bucket and came walking out the door. He came by the sheriff, saying in a womanish voice, "Good evening, Mr. Dodd. Nice evening."

Then the man walked on to the barn caught the horse and rode out the back way through the woods, while the sheriff waited patiently for him to come out of the house.

Whether this man stole the horse or not is not known. His owner found the horse in his barn lot the next morning and the warrant was withdrawn.

There are others like the human coon dog of Capses Gap. But space forbids writing about them—besides this is Thanksgiving night, and I've just eaten a holiday supper of turkey and old ham and all the other good things—thanks to our daughter, Mrs. Bradley of Clearview who sent it.

Included in all these good things was a baked Irish potato with the jacket on. I wondered why she sent that, then I figured out and found myself in the same boat with the old farmer's wife who escorted her little 5-year old daughter to school her first day. The teacher asked the lady when the little girl's birthday was and she answered, "Well, she was born in tater time. But I just can't remember—whether it wus plantin' 'em or diggn' 'em."

April 7, 1966
Gazette & Star News

Billy the Goat's Tales of Two Towns By L. D. R.

I once knew a charming young lady named May. She had a beau—a nice fellow, all right—but we always called him "April Showers," because he brought May flowers.

April is here again, and we need the showers or else there will be few flowers.

Wonder how many of you ever ate an "April Fool" dinner? I have—after pulling a few shenanigans to get it cooked. That happened nearly three score years ago—when, as a school boy, I was always hungry.

At that time I was attending school in Nashville, but I was always homesick for the hills and open spaces. On weekends I came home to get the news, and lucky I was to have a way home back then. Train fare home and back was 70 cents, and that was the only way of getting home except walking.

The news in Long Hollow one weekend was fantastic! Aunt Betty had a beau! Ever since we kids were knee-high to a duck she had never had one. We had heard that long before we were born she had refused to marry her childhood sweetheart because he wanted to take her to Arkansas to live, and she didn't want to leave her mother and move that far away.

What made it so exciting to us was the fact that she was the only aunt we had, and it seemed she was going to be ours for keeps. Even when this venerable old squire in the upper reaches of the county wrote her a letter asking her for a date she refused, because she still didn't want to leave her mother who was now 80.

Grandmother was sick and her two widowed sisters were with her to help wait on her. The next morning I went up to see her, but nothing was said about Aunt Betty's would-be suitor. Suddenly I remembered it was April 1, so I rushed back home in a hurry.

Enlisting the help of two of my sisters, we found a valentine card with a Fountain Head postmark on it, which was the Squire's post office. We changed the date to April 1, erased the other writing on it, than with a pencil printed this on the card: *"Dear Miss Betty, this is to tell you that I will be at your house Sunday, April 2, to eat dinner with you."*

Signed, J. W. Simpson

Then along came Charlie Wilhoite, our obliging mail carrier. We let him in on the joke, and he was tickled to deliver it for us.

Then sister Myrtle went up to the mail box. The card was read and business picked up in that old kitchen. Myrtle was kept to help. A hen was dressed and a cake was baked. One of the aunts, who knew the old gentleman, was let in on the secret. But Grandmother and her other sister were kept in the dark about all the goings on.

Later on that day our own mother visited Grandmother, and told her not to worry—that it was just an April Fool's joke. Amazingly, that sick old lady never gave the secret away, but had a big laugh out of it.

After Sunday School the next day, the four of us grandsons invited ourselves to Grandmother's house for dinner. Aunt Betty waited dinner until 2:00 o'clock, then decided her beau was not coming, and she let us eat. Well, she got the biggest surprise of her life when we devilish nephews began passing the food to one another, saying, "have some of the chicken, Mr. Simpson."

Then she caught on, and we all began laughing, causing Grandmother to call out from her sick bed, "I knew all the time it was an April Fool. But it's good enough for you—you should have let him come the first time he asked."

Well, the next day another letter came from Squire Simpson, asking for a date the following Sunday. Aunt Betty gladly answered, telling him he was welcome and that she had already cooked one dinner for him and could cook another.

Just a few weeks later, they were married and lived happily ever after.

It was a year or two before I had the pleasure of meeting my new uncle, because I was working in the city. Although, every time they visited Long Hollow he asked about the boy who wrote the card.

Finally I boarded a train at Union Station with a ticket to Fountain Head. When I reached his house, he was in the field at work. Shortly he came in and Aunt Betty told him, "Here is that mischievous nephew you have been wanting to see."

I shall never forget what he said to me as he shook my hand, "Boy—if you hadn't broken the ice for me I never would have gotten her."

May 12, 1966
Gazette & Star News

Billy the Goat's
Tales of Two Towns
By L. D. R.

People today live fast, with cars and big trucks running bumper to bumper on all the highways. They have to be fast to get out of the way and live at all.

But I like to turn the calendar back three score years and remember how much more colorful life was back then, when you had time to stop and look at it.

Take, for instance, a big load of lumber that would make the trucks today look like midgets, turning off Long Hollow Pike into Two Mile Pike. This giant wagon is pulled by four big mules and Pap Sprouse is sitting in the saddle on the back of the lead mule. Ab Watkins, a teamster, is following right behind with another four-mule team and a load just like the first. Dorris Brothers Milling Company is sending the first lumber that was ever unloaded on the grounds to help build Madison Sanitarium.

The two veteran drivers will get there before sundown, unload their wagons, feed their teams, then sleep on the ground in a buck bush patch. In the morning they will hitch up their teams and leisurely make their way back to Capses Gap. People back then didn't try to do it all in one day. They took their time and enjoyed life.

On Thursdays you will hear a bugle blowing as it comes down the pike, but it won't be Gabriel. Jim Garrison, driving two little mules to a covered wagon, will be using the bugle to call all the housewives to bring out their chickens and eggs and butter to sell, so he can help feed Nashville.

Come summer time, and you'll see a bunch of kids hanging out on the front yard fence, looking expectantly up the road. Then you know they have heard a wildcat whistle blowing on a traction engine and are eagerly awaiting it to come into view pulling a big cyclone thresher, painted up in bright colors. Watch until it gets close to the kids and you'll see the fireman stoke some broken fence rails in the firebox to get up plenty of steam, because he knows that when the engineer gets to the kids on the fence, he is going to pull that wildcat whistle wide open and scare the daylights out of them, running the girls back in the house and making the hair on all the boys' heads stand straight up.

Find something today that will attract the kids away from television and get out where the front yard fence ought to be. More than likely it would have to be something like Father Time, with his long white beard driving a team of oxen to a prairie schooner, which you'd be obliged to borrow from the past.

A trip to Nashville used to be a thrill instead of a headache. There was nothing to fear as long as you kept out of reach of the thundering hooves of the fire engine horses. There were wagons hauling produce to town the year around, but in the summer they increased greatly in number.

There was Cousin Browny, for instance, who was called that only as a nick-name, because when he was a boy his daddy, who had to act as both mother and father to him, made him a pair of pants with one leg out of gray jeans and the other out of brown. As soon as poke sallet poked up out of the ground in the Spring, Browny and his partner would start their treks to town and continue through all the seasons, including the rabbit season. They often had to spend the night in town, and when they did, they always took in the Princess Theatre. Browny would come back to Shackle Island telling fantastic tales about the shows they had seen.

Once, though, they gave him the horse laugh, because when he was asked what the admission was, he answered, "Just a couple of buffaloes."

They thought he didn't know what "admission" meant, but he did, referring to nickels as "buffaloes."

Once they carried with them Jimmy Hullem, a middle-aged back-woodsman who had never seen a movie. When the show started that night, a train, big as the real thing, came roaring around a curve on the screen and looked like it was heading straight for the audience. Jimmy jumped up and ran out the door, like a rabbit a dog was chasing.

Then there was the Shackle Island boy who was an expert at playing jokes on the sundry citizens of that little village. This boy made his first trip to Nashville alone to visit some old school mates who were staying there. These friends met him at old Link's Depot and the first thing he said as he stepped off the train was, "Boys, let's go to the Princess." They all agreed.

When the leader neared the Arcade, he said, "Get your dime out, boys, Here's where you pay." Then he walked on to where a Salvation Army lady was ringing a bell and dropped a coin in the pot. Following, this joker from Shackle Island walked by and dropped in his dime, also.

When all of them walked out of the other end of the Arcade, the boy was astounded, and he knew he had been played for a sucker.

Such was life back in days gone by.

July 28, 1966
Gazette & Star News

Billy the Goat's
Tales of Two Towns
By L. D. R.

Riches are something everyone should have if possible. The ones that don't have such are very unfortunate. As for me, I've been rich all my life. Yes, that is a fact, for thank goodness I've always had good health, lots of friends and only once in my life have I had less than five cents in my pocket. Here are some of the episodes that have made me rich:

On Thanksgiving Day, 1912, I went rabbit hunting in a canyon at the foot of the Rockies. Soon I decided to go up on the mountain. There I found myself looking for mountain lions, not to shoot at them but to stay out of their way. When I feared the lion was stalking me from behind, I went down on the other side and came to Turkey Creek. From there I had to go down the creek a few miles to get around the mountain. Soon I came to a small field of rye, fenced with barb wire, that I had to cross or else wade the creek or again climb the mountain, so I got over the fence and started across when a big red heifer, out of a bunch of cows grazing there, came charging at me with her long horns lowered toward the ground. Well, I couldn't shoot that cow in her own private pasture so I vaulted that fence, shotgun and all, and saved my life. Then I scrambled around the edge of the mountain to the other side.

Later that winter when the weather got down to 20 below and the work all shut down, I was laid off until March and told to go back to Pueblo and pick-up odd jobs. The striking part of this story is that the manager of the store, that they all told me I couldn't get along with, I had made a friend out of and he insisted that I come back in the Spring. Destiny, though, decreed that I didn't go back.

In Pueblo I got a temporary job at a furniture store until one of their hands recovered from blood poisoning. I was put to work as a helper on the delivery wagon. Edwards, from Kentucky, was the driver and became my good friend. The first thing we delivered was a piano. When we started up a narrow stairway with it "a woman" up at the top began screaming, "Help, Help, Murder," and I was visibly perturbed. Edwards saw I was upset and laughed, telling me it was an old parrot.

Late Saturday afternoon we were sent out to Bessemer, a suburb five miles away, to deliver a load of furniture. We were long after dark getting through and Edward told me not to stop at the office to get my pay because the sick man had returned to work that morning and they were going to lay me off. He said, "Come back to work on Monday," and I could make another day which I did. I thanked him for his friendly advice. However, he lived in Bessemer and kept the wagon and team there, so I had to catch a street car back to town. When I started to pay my fare I found I'd lost my pocketbook. I offered to pawn my watch to the driver, but he said, "No, just drop a nickel in the box up on the street near the store, the first time you pass it." I did and became convinced that a friend is worth more than all the money in the world. Oh, yes, I found my pocketbook when I reached my room.

This town was an important railroad center, having a number of lines running into it. So I got a job in the Denver and Rio Grande freight yards. I didn't work regularly. During the time I was, I acquired a lot of friends, heard a lot of talk about rains and railroads, and was informed that a fellow could always find a good job in Kansas City.

The West at that time was a long way from Shackle Island, with only one way to get there and that was by train, which meant doing without the luxuries of life a long time to save money to buy a ticket.

Arriving back home a year or so later people were curious about how fast these western trains run, so I told them this one to illustrate. Departing for Kansas City to find a better job, I rode the Missouri Pacific. Somewhere in Kansas this train made a brief stop and a woman came driving up in a buggy, bringing her husband to catch the train. They both jumped out and the lady stood by the train while her husband tugged two suitcases aboard and disposed of them, then darted back out to kiss his wife goodbye. This fellow seemed unaware that the very moment he got aboard, the train started moving and was speeding Eastward like a streak. He swung down on the bottom step and puckered up to kiss her and kissed a cow right in the mouth. The cow was standing by the track nine miles from where he left his wife.

Arriving in Kansas City around noon that Saturday, I got off the train and walked down the street a block or two and came to a big wholesale seed house where I met the shipping clerk. He was just returning from lunch. "Where can I find a job?" I asked. "Be here Monday morning at 7 and I'll put you to work," he answered as he stepped inside the building. Monday morning I was waiting when he came to open for business. I found him to be no hard taskmaster if you did as you were instructed to do. If you didn't he would cuss you out.

A few days later he gave me a scoop and told me to unload 80 thousand pounds of sorghum seed into an elevator beside the big box car. It took me most of the day and he came in as I finished and found no fault in my work. He told me to have nothing to do with the rest of the gang that worked there

and to never loan them money to go out and get drunk on.

One day I was down in the basement after a sack of seed corn and I pulled the elevator out from under one of this gang as he stepped on it pulling a heavy 4-wheeled truck. The poor fellow was a white as a sheet and badly scared. I helped him load his truck with a dozen bags of potatoes, then we both pulled our trucks on the elevator and I moved it up to the main floor expecting to get a cussing.

The boss' desk was right beside the elevator and he looked up and cussed that fellow until I felt sorry for him. He called him a drunken fool who was going to get his neck broken because I had rung the bell twice to keep anyone off and he had heard it, he said.

There was one of the gang that was always telling the boss how they did things over at Rudy's, another seed house. He and I were emptying sacks of grain into a machine that carried it to the top floor, when I dropped a grain sack into the maw of the machine. I asked the boss how to get it out and he flew into a rage and asked, "Did that damn fool drop a sack in there?" I quickly told him I did it myself and he stopped cussing and pointed to a long stick with a hook on it to get out the sack and cautioned me to be careful.

Three of this gang, all twice my age, were continually making all manner of fun of me. I took it all and never complained to anyone about it. I was just biding my time to even things up. One day they asked what crops we grew in Tennessee. I told them the main crop was tobacco and that I had a problem I wanted them to solve for me. I drew a crude map of a long river with three small animals on one side and some vegetation on the other and told them there was a tobacco patch loaded with big green horn worms. Three polecats across the river wanted to get across to eat them, but they couldn't swim and there was no bridge. The problem—How were they going to do it? After this gang had studied the problem awhile I asked, "Do you all three give up?" They answered "Yes." "That's exactly what the other three polecats did," I informed them.

Sandy, the machinist, overheard this and told me later how it tickled him because they were always picking on me and that it would break them from doing it. Sure enough, it did.

This is the story except that when my friend with whom I went west stopped in Kansas City to get me to come back to Tennessee with him, my boss told him he would never have told him I was there had he known what my friend wanted. I was the only employee he had he could depend on.

All you have read happened more than 50 years ago today. I'm still rich because every friend who reads this column is more valuable to me than a million dollars.

August 4, 1966
Gazette & Star News

Billy the Goat's Tales of Two Towns By L. D. R.

In these days when peacemakers are needed greatly, a story about an unusual peacemaker has drawn my attention.

Max lives in Springfield. He is half shepherd and half collie and belongs to our little grandson. Nearby is another dog of the same cross breed and also a big collie. Every time these three get together they have a fight and a water hose has to be turned on them to get them to stop. Little granddaughter Susie has a year old fawn colored cat—a long bodied, short-haired cat of Asiatic ancestry that looks more like a wild animal than a house cat. The other day these dogs got into a big fight, the two smaller ones getting the big collie down and gnawing on his throat, when up came this tom cat. He jumped right on top of all three with all his might.

This doesn't sound reasonable, but the dogs were scared so badly they all jumped up and scattered. The neighbors across the street were looking on, and they said they never saw anything like it.

In all the fights I have ever seen there has always been a peacemaker. For instance, the preacher who was preaching right in the middle of the side street near the main thoroughfare over fifty years ago. He asked his listeners to quit blowing cigarette smoke in his face. He asked them a second time, and when they didn't quit, he yelled, "I can whip any cigarette smoker in this town."

Some fellow on the outer edge of the crowd yelled back, "Old man, you are taking in too much territory."

Immediately, the preacher threw off his coat, rolled up his sleeves and said, "If you want to fight, come on."

They hit one another with their fists several times and were getting warmed up for a real fight when an interfering peacemaker in a policeman's uniform walked up and stopped them, and carried them away in a horse drawn paddy wagon. And there I stood all disappointed, because I wanted to see if this preacher could do what he said he could do.

However, all fights don't turn out like that one. Only a few years before this I witnessed a fight where the peacemaker got nabbed. This happened at old Winthrop School in Nashville one cold day when we boys were eating lunch. We were upstairs in the chapel with the doors closed, when two bantam rooster type boys, about 16 and built like bulldogs, got into a fight. An older boy, a tall fellow from a place called Goodlettsville intervened to stop the brawl. However, there was another boy there, older and taller than this fellow—a 25-year old Indian from Oklahoma who locked his arms around the peacemaker and exclaimed, "Let 'em fight—I've got Sister."

And that they did, until both of them became exhausted and had to stop. Then the Indian ordered them to shake hands and smoke the pipe of peace. This was one fight the faculty never knew about, for no one dared tell because the Indian refereed it, and he was bigger than any of us.

With all the strife and turmoil in the world today, no one seems to have the technique to stop it like the old-timers had in bygone days. Take, for instance, the technique used by a certain Shackle Island merchant. One day a contentious fellow made the mistake of getting involved in an argument with a fellow who would fight and who was just in the right mood that day. This fellow advanced on the contentious one with his knife open. The merchant not wanting any blood shed in this store, picked up a chair and knocked the attacker cold and sprawled on the floor. This incident occurred about 75 years ago, before I was old enough to remember it. But for all these many years, I hear this same fellow has been grateful.

How many people in this world do you think it would help to have an old split bottom chair swung at their heads to knock some peaceful thoughts into their noggins, and fights and strikes and riots out of them? And how many need a tom cat to jump on their backs and start scratching until they stop itching for more of this world's goods and become satisfied with what they have?

January 12, 1967
Goodlettsville Gazette

Billy the Goat's Tales of Two Towns By L. D. R.

This week the column is being written in the form of a letter to my Cousin Mrs. Ethel Hanson of Yakima, Washington, whose grandfather, a Ralph of Shackle Island, married a Kizer and moved west with her a 100 years ago or more. She is the daughter of the late James Ralph of Nevada. I have never seen her or her niece, Mrs. John Sharp of Elko, Nevada, who started our correspondence a few years ago seeking information for a family tree.

Dear Ethel:

I am writing you to tell you about your father's first cousins here in Tennessee (Joan will get a copy, too). They are all dead now, but were prominent citizens.

First, there was Cousin Nora, who was a very religious lady. When the minister preached her funeral a few years ago he said that when Miss Nora died all the religion of that 140 year old rock church died with her. He told the truth, because no one has shouted in the old church since.

She was a very remarkable woman. Her tongue was the nearest thing to perpetual motion ever created. She never stopped talking. I remember when I was a boy, Uncle Sumner Ralph had a corn crop on the farm belonging to her and her sister, and I was hired to help work it. As we drove up the lane toward their farm, Uncle Sumner got off the wagon to talk to another farmer, and his boys and I drove on to the field. When I was opening the gate in front of their house Cousin Nora poked her head out the front door and Cousin Laura poked her head out the kitchen door, and in unison screamed, "Law, where is Summy?"

Just for pure mischief I answered, "He's been summoned to Gallatin on the Kizer trial."

Well, I never heard anything like it before or since. They preached all the Kizers' funerals from A to Izzard, and were still preaching when we reached the field. Then they hushed, but about 15 minutes later started preaching again louder than ever, and I knew what had happened. Soon Uncle Summy came up grinning, and said, "You need never worry about having your funeral preached—them two are preaching it now."

The funny thing about it was the Kizer trial was held half a dozen years before this happened, and was the most spectacular trial ever held in that old courthouse. Uncle Mark, your grandmother's old Gallatin bachelor brother, had died, leaving a fine farm and a truck full of money. Cousin Lizzie, your father's double first cousin, had lived with her uncle and cared for him most of her life. The trial was between her and the rest of the heirs.

The man, however, who was between the devil and the deep blue sea, was the Sheriff of Sumner County, Frank Patton. He had to keep his kinsmen from being fined for contempt of court when they got to wrangling with each other before the judge. Frank, too, was your father's first cousin.

Incidentally, Cousin Lizzie's heirs own the farm today, for the verdict of the jury was in her favor.

About 10 years after having my funeral preached, I quit lying and became a carpenter, and these two dear spinsters who preached it, employed me to remodel their old colonial house. At the time I owned a rubber-tired buggy and a nice horse. A revival was being held at the old rock church a mile away. One day I asked these ladies who a pretty little plump girl was whom I saw at church the night before, and I was told. That evening about sundown when I had just changed my clothes for church those two ladies began to yell, "Here comes Hester!" She was with a gang of youngsters walking to church.

I got a double introduction to her. Both these ladies were talking at the same time. I went on to church with her and later carried her back home in my buggy after the service. It was a case of love at first sight. She fell in love with the horse and buggy, and must have decided that night she was going to own them, even though she had to agree to make biscuits for a hard-headed man for the next 50 years.

Well, she was driving this outfit back home before the next revival and calling it her own, and I reckon it was, for she only lacks until April 8th this very year having it paid for.

Hester and I naturally have been grateful to Cousin Nora for the part she played in our lives, but about 30 years later our good deeds backfired. We had brought her home with us for dinner the Sunday the revival started that year, and she evidently appreciated the dinner she had. Anyway, at services that night she jumped up and began shouting—and around through the pulpit she came and on to me with her arms spread wide to hug me. But in a split second I kicked the chair out from under me and fell to the floor, then darted out a side door, missing her embrace by a gnat's bristle.

She shouted, "Law, he's gone!" And everybody laughed, except one long-faced lady who later told me I acted awfully ugly.

Maybe my conscious would still be hurting me for the way I did our shouting cousin had not the lady evangelist, a spinster herself, visited us the very next day and exonerated me. She said she witnessed the whole act, and that I did exactly the right thing by not letting her hug me.

Now a word more about the Kizers: One of these first cousins owned the best kept farm in the county. On his level fields and

rolling pastures he never allowed a bush, briar or weed to grow.

But being a perfectionist doesn't warrant him space in this column. This does, however:

One cold night he and his wife walked across the pastures to a social at a neighbor's house. Back then the punch served on such occasions was 100 proof out of a jug, and this cousin got his share of it. Returning home, he started to build a fire in the open fireplace, but instead of laying the wood across the dog irons in the conventional manner, he stood it upright with one end sticking up the chimney.

When his wife saw him she said, "Put that wood on there right, sir!"

This was his answer, which is now a by-word around Shackle Island: "Oh, no burn it the way it grows!"

Another cousin, the quickest thinking of all, owned only an acre of ground with a house on it, and it full of children. He had a couple of stands of bees. One day he robbed them and got a few buckets of honey. Then, catching a ride to Nashville, he carried some of the honey with him to sell on the farmer's market. He had sold all but one bucket when a chain store buyer came along, and he tried to sell the buyer that bucket.

But the big business man made all manner of fun and asked, "Is that all the honey you have, you one-horse farmer, you?"

By quick thinking your cousin answered, "No, sir. I have about 150 pounds at home as pretty as you ever laid eyes on."

Well, it turned out the buyer bought the one bucket, and said he would stop and look at what the cousin had at home if the honey in the bucket suited.

Evidently it did, for a few mornings later the buyer stopped his car in front of Cousin Bee's house and came blustering in calling out, "All right, Honey Bee, I want to see that mass of honey you bragged about."

"Good lady!" the shrewd Bee called out, and his attractive wife appeared in the doorway. Then he said to the buyer, "There she is—look at her."

You regular readers can say these stories are re-runs if you wish. But it had to be so that Joan can place these illustrious cousins high on her family tree, as shining lights from Tennessee.

July 13, 1967
Goodlettsville Gazette

Billy the Goat's Tales of Two Towns By L. D. R.

This paper sure does go places; just got word from Pakistan where Robert Worsham is stationed in the armed services. He writes his mother that he reads this column and enjoys it.

Robert is from Shackle Island, so it sounds proper to tell a few tall tales, as one lady calls them, about his home town. It is the 4th of July and people are wondering what kind of winter this is where we have to sleep under heavy quilts every night.

To me it is shorts' winter, which comes every summer immediately after the queen of this steep and rugged domain decrees that I wear sleazy calico shorts under my pants the rest of the summer. It's going to be freeze and sneeze until the first snow.

Last week it was hot but luckily I still had on long handles when I went out on the farm one afternoon after coming home from work. I was bent on picking $5 worth of blackberries. I had two quart cups full in the small basket swinging on my belt when I stumbled and fell backwards into a big briar patch. There I lay flat on my back and head down hill. I couldn't move for the briars held me firmly. Soon I became wringing wet with sweat and was about to cook. But like a worm on a hot griddle, I began to squirm and wiggle and got my feet down hill, then crawled out and cooled off.

The amazing thing was that although I spilled my two quarts of berries, I never got a scratch. The long handles kept the briars from perforating me and made me sweat to kill all the chiggers.

I kept picking and picked eight quarts more which I sold to the supermarket. Now, you may wonder why a fellow that was three score and ten long enough ago to have the seven-year itch and be well of it, keeps on picking berries. Well, the truth of it is success has finally caught up with me, for when I was ten years old I picked a six-gallon crate one day and sold it for sixty cents. Today I can pick that many and sell them for $12 which is twenty times what I got for the first ones.

Here is a story that has never been told before, that this far-away soldier's grandfather played a major part in. Almost three score years ago, there was a secret order called the Shackle Island Board of Health. The address was Democratic Building, Room 6, 10th floor. J. Proctor Knott was president and John Randolph Wilkerson was secretary. None of these ever existed and the place these mischievous boys hung out and planned their pranks was this grandfather's store. He never aided or abetted the boys, but he never once squealed on them about anything.

At that time, there was an old two story brick house, plus full-size basement and attic, that no one had lived in for years. Then one summer, a light began appearing on dark nights on the roof of the old house. What sounded like a woman's voice would scream some very unearthly screams. Women in the neighborhood became frightened and wouldn't walk by it, even in the daytime. Like everything else that took place, others laid it to a prank of the Board of Health.

The merchant then told these boys that they had double-crossed him, by scaring all his women customers and causing them to go around the other road and trade at the other store. But the boys denied having anything to do with it. Then he said, "Put a stop to it, and I'll believe you."

The first thing the Board of Health did was case the old house and discover that the "Ghost" that waved the lantern on top got up there by entering through a small basement window. It would then go up a stairway to the spacious hall, on up the broad stairway to the second story, then up a small stairway to the attic, and on up a ladder to a trap door on the roof.

They made elaborate plans to scare the dickens out of the prowler and also find out who he was even though it was pitch dark throughout the building. Three charter members of the Board were to slip in and up to the top of the main stairway before the "ghost" arrived. With them, one boy brought his big Newfoundland dog to leave with the other two. The dog wore a big log chain fastened around his collar to hold him by, while his master descended back to the basement. He would whistle to the dog to make him ready to come back down, when the chain was released, as the victim got half way up the steps.

It would have been nip and tuck between the dog dragging the log chain down the steps to get to his master in the basement and the "ghost" to get out the basement window. But luckily for "ghost" and to the disappointment of the three boys, someone had told him that the Board of Health had a trap set for him and he never did come back to wave a lantern and scream like a woman in distress on the roof of the ancient building.

That is the story of a drama that didn't work out as planned. It would have made big headlines around Shackle Island.

The Board of Health also had a diabolical plan to identify their victim had things worked out as they planned. The boys in the basement had an improvised pair of pinchers made by nailing two tobacco sticks together with two sharp nails protruding through each of the pincher parts of the devise. When the victim started scrambling out the narrow window, he was going to grab his leg with these pinchers, tear his pants and leave a wound that looked like it was made by dog teeth.

The next day, they intended to go to the keeper of the community mad stone, that everybody used back then to keep from having hydrophobia, and find out who borrowed it the night before.

For more than half a century, this ingenious plan that failed has troubled my mind. Had it succeeded, the town criers would have had a golden jubilee, like they did after every other sanitary act by the Board of Health.

For instance, when a very prominent citizen allowed his horses to graze along the public highway at night, he found them two days later in a farmer's back pasture, busy grazing away. But not before he had called the sheriffs of several adjoining counties and told them to be on the lookout for three stolen horses.

July 20, 1967
Goodlettsville Gazette

Billy the Goat's
Tales of Two Towns
By L. D. R.

Last week this column told about the Old Brick at Shackle Island and things that once happened there, so it is only fair to tell about the great rock castle that stands across the creek nearby and the devilment the youngsters got into at this very place when I was a boy. You readers can be the judge and jury too, to decide just how guilty they were.

First, a word about the notorious band of boys' and girls' auxiliaries that made them click. The young fellow that organized this secret order was a polite serious-minded youngster beyond suspicion that many mothers in the community pointed to for their sons to be more like. In fact, he was held in such high esteem that disgruntled victims of these boys' pranks sometimes came to this very young fellow and offered him money to find out for them who the pranksters were. Of course, he would tell them he would do all he could to find out who they were. And then he would dictate a nice letter to the complainants telling them—we understand you have grown very indignant over certain things that have been done to you. We assure you we are very sorry, but the health of this community demanded that they be done so we were only performing our duty—signed Shackle Island Board of Health, John Randolph Wilkerson, Sec., J. Proctor Knott, Pres. The handwriting didn't give any clue as to the writer because they were rewritten by a penmanship expert in Nashville. However, the complainant would bring the letter to this young "innocent" fellow and offer him five dollars more to find

out who these two birds were that signed the letter they received.

Back now to the old rock castle. It was on a fine creek bottom farm and the elderly man and wife who owned it and lived there were splendid people, who frowned on extravagance. So when we asked them to let us have a party there they agreed to furnish the refreshments but didn't say what they wanted us to get to serve. So, it being a tacky party, we bought a half bushel of roasted peanuts in the hull and sent them to their home the afternoon before the party. That night we all gathered with no intention whatever of getting into mischief because we all held great respect for anyone who befriended us; besides we never premeditated anything in advance.

There were eighty-one guests present and it was after eight o'clock old time and no peanuts had been passed around. Then one of the five charter members of the Board chanced to step out into the spacious hall and heard the hostess balling out two younger boys for trying to find the peanuts. Then she exclaimed loudly, "You are not going to have them, you'll get hulls all over the floor. I've locked them up in the kitchen and have the key in my pocket and double dare anybody to get them."

J. Proctor Knott was sitting in the far corner of the big parlor busy talking to his girl when the hostess' words were relayed to him.

"Show me the kitchen," he said as he arose and followed his informant out the front hall door to retrieve the peanuts that were locked up inside that solid eighteen inch wall. In a minute's time he had the big sack of peanuts in his hand and started back inside. Three more boys were standing outside so the five of them, by filling all their pants and coats pockets emptied the sack and re-entered the parlor and began handing peanuts to all with orders to not allow a hull to fall to the floor. The hostess, of course, at this time was in the living room across the hall entertaining some older guests. Later when we all left for home, we told her truthfully what an enjoyable time we all had, so perhaps she felt relieved that none of us were sore about her not letting us have our own peanuts.

Perhaps the next morning when she entered the kitchen and found the sack of peanuts gone from off the kitchen table, she plum forgot the window had no lock on it and thought the mice got them and carried the cloth sack along with them to make bedding. Anyway, she probably became convinced the mice carried them away when later she found the hulls neatly stored in the dresser drawers and elsewhere in the parlor.

Well, readers of the jury, you have heard the case. What is your verdict? Is it right or wrong to steal your own property and prove that you could keep the hulls off the floor?

Of all things, here is an unusual request from a reader. At our celebration a Nashville businessman formerly of Shackle Island shook hands with me and said he reads the column every week. He then told me to put something in here about his daddy. He said that would get him. Well, this column is not out to get anybody, besides, his daddy and I have been life-long friends regardless of all that has transpired between us.

I remember well the first time we met. It was one Monday morning and he was about knee high to a duck and I was a year or so older. He was a pilot in a cow barn and had piled up great conical piles of dry dust in the cow shed.

He bet me a nickel that I couldn't stand five feet away and jump on top of one of these heaps of dry dust. I jumped and landed smack dab on top of the pile, but it wasn't dry down underneath and my feet flew out from under me and I sat right down in the stuff.

However, life is too short to hold a grudge against a fellow for playing dirty jokes on you, so dirty that my clean clothes were ruined.

You just forget it, for eventually he will get you in a crowd and try to pull another one on you and sooner or later he will hand you his empty shotgun, then throw up his hat for you to shoot at, so they can all laugh at you when you take aim and pull the trigger and the gun falls to fire, leaving you standing there looking like a fool.

So, to avoid such, always have a loaded shotgun shell in your pocket which you slip in the gun when he turns around to wink at the others. Then all he can say is "Phaw, I didn't think that gun was loaded."

So, believe it or not a fellow going home bare-headed back then was something to laugh about.

September 7, 1967
Gazette and Star News

Billy the Goat's
Tales of Two Towns
By L. D. R.

Probably by the time you read this you will also have read about the president's election over in Vietnam.

I'd like to give you a few reasons people vote. A few have a personal friend, and they vote for him regardless, while half of the others vote for the candidate that some notorious element they don't like is against. Then the other half votes against the man this group is supporting—that is politics.

Recently we read in the papers about some fiery leaders of the minority group who have adopted that very policy to elect the man they want. They are admonishing their followers to vote against President Johnson, their best friend, knowing the vast majority of voters will be for him, and elect him, because they are seemingly against him.

Then they go still further and advise their followers to vote for George Wallace, knowing full well that if they can convince people they are for Wallace, he will be defeated. So don't let them pull the wool over your eyes.

Now, if you don't believe this is the way to win and election, listen to this:

Many years ago Mr. Manier, a fine old gentleman, lived up Madison Creek, and didn't take any stock in politics. I arrived at the Bloody Six voting precinct in my old car just 30 minutes before time for the polls to close, and asked if this old gentleman had been out to vote. Several men told me he hadn't and that they had sent after him a half dozen times and he wouldn't come. They said I needn't go after him.

"He will come when I go after him," I told them, as I cranked my old car. They all laughed at me like they thought I was a fool.

When I arrived at the old fellow's home, he was throwing his saddle on his horse to go after the cows.

"Don't buckle that saddle, I'm taking you to the polls to vote," I shouted. He looked at me and said, "Aw, why do you want me to vote?"

I answered, "Squire Jackson says if Hub Perdue carries this district he will move out of it."

Instantly, he jerked the saddle off and said, "Let's go."

So that was one more vote Hub got because the Squire had given judgment against this honorable old famer.

Elections back then, before voters had to register to vote, were much more colorful than they are today and just as fair, according to the old adage, "What's good for the goose, is good for the gander, too."

In all my born days, there has never been but two men elected sheriff of Sumner County from this end of the county. "Old Big Foot" was elected sheriff from the Bloody Six before I was old enough to vote. He was nicknamed that by the law breakers of the county, because he could out run all of them in a foot race and never pull his gun on them. He made a good sheriff and when he retired, his chief deputy from Hendersonville ran and Big Foot saw to it that he was elected. There was a crop of boys who had just become old enough to vote for the first time; the amiable old sheriff told these boys to go to Shackle Island in the seventh and vote, giving their initials. Then come back to their district, where he voted them by their full name.

These boys didn't think there was any harm in doing it, because all their lives they had heard that a train load of voters came from Kentucky and voted for the candidate from the other end of the county every election day.

Then there was Hannibal Patton, a bearded colored man, who I barely remember as the most polite man I ever met. He always voted, but had already passed away by this election day. "Who would Uncle Hannibal vote for if he was living," someone would say. "He'd vote for Bowles," another would answer. "Let's vote him then," the judges would sing out.

But this old fellow was not the only tombstone that voted there that day by a long jump. For Madison Creek sent in more votes than South Tunnel and Bowles was elected sheriff and served with distinction.

However, even though registering to vote wasn't required then, Shackle Island had one man they couldn't beat by hook or crook. He was a noted orator who could make a speech on any subject and hold his audience spellbound. He was also a great diplomat who, to rich and poor alike, was always saying something complimentary to make them feel better.

He was the honorable D. A. Montgomery, an old school teacher of mine, who ran for magistrate of the seventh district four times, and for state representative from Sumner County three times. He got every vote in his district every time he ran.

Not withstanding all of this, this man had a temper that, when stirred up, the fat was in the fire.

The first time he ran for representative, his lawyer opponent challenged him to meet him in debate in the lawyer's own district in the upper end of the county.

Driving the twenty-five miles to meet his opponent, this diplomatic fellow fully intended to say nothing but nice things about his opponent. But the lawyer, who spoke first, made the mistake of calling this man of good intentions "a little one-horse farmer from Shackle Island."

Then came the one-horse fellow's time to speak. He had his dander up, and he told how proud he was of his heritage as a farmer who knew the problems of an agricultural county. He then asked what a lawyer would know about such problems and further ridiculed the lawyer so much that when the votes were counted, he beat the lawyer in his own district and won a landslide victory all over the county!

I once voted for a fellow for constable because I thought that would be the only vote he would get in our precinct, but all the others thought the same thing, and this fellow was elected.

Many, many years ago, Uncle Alec was a poor, droll farmer who couldn't read or write, who for a joke somebody persuaded him to do, ran for magistrate against Captain Waters, the rich merchant and timber buyer who had held office ever since the Civil War.

The Captain got a big laugh out of it when he said to Uncle Alec, "They tell me you are running against me." "Yes, Captain, and I'm gonna walk ye log," answered Uncle Alec.

The Captain didn't laugh, though when the votes were counted for the jokers had elected Alec, who served out his term by having his daughter do his reading and writing for him.

So vote and time will tell whether you voted right or wrong.

September 21, 1967
Goodlettsville Gazette

Billy the Goat's Tales of Two Towns By L. D. R.

Most of the time if something unusual happens at Shackle Island you go to Shackle Island to find out all about it. But I have just found that for once that method isn't working, and I am still in the dark about the information I am seeking.

Word has just come to me from the Pope in Rome that a meteorite once fell near Drakes Creek in Sumner County, and is now in the Vatican in possession of the Pope.

Records have been kept that Spencer was Sumner County's first settler and that he lived in a hollow sycamore tree on the banks of the Cumberland near Castalian Springs.

At the sesquicentennial held in Gallatin some 30 odd years ago there was a very impressive float in the parade which was witnessed by me and all my family. It was a large flat-bottomed truck with a monstrous hollow sycamore stump about eight feet high on it. By the stump was a man representing Spencer dressed in coonskin clothes and cooking a meal over an open fire. My family was in a pageant given by Shackle Island that day. Gov. Gordon Browning spoke on the Trousdale House balcony, and as he was winding up his speech, great crowds assembled on each side of the walkway ready to shake hands with the Governor when he departed for the capitol in Nashville.

However, it seemed the Governor didn't care to shake hands with so many people. The instant he stopped speaking, he darted across the balcony to the end where he stepped over the banister and headed straight across the side lawn to where I was standing holding Wallace, our youngest, in my arms. The Chief of State patted the baby boy on the back and shook hands with me and was gone.

Now back to the original subject:

Caspar Mansker was Goodlettsville's first settler. The creek there was named for him and they have bronze markers there telling about him. Since there have been records kept of these historical happenings and most others in the area, my question is this: When a heavenly body descended at Shackle Island, why didn't our ancestors leave some record of it? We'd like to know when and where it fell, and also what kind of a display it made when coming down to earth.

Perhaps some of you readers can furnish us some interesting information about this meteor. My son-in-law, Ollie Smith, Jr., is a geologist and would like very much to hear more about it. He also suggested that I write about it.

According to the Pope's information, this meteorite fell in 1823. The old rock church at Shackle Island was built in 1828, and many of us have heard all our lives that the first stove in the church was bought with money from the sale of that meteor. But that is all any of us know about it, so it seems strange that we have to depend on word from the Vatican across the ocean to learn what year it fell.

I got this latest information about the matter from Ollie Smith, Sr., who bought a meteor several years ago that had fallen near Mayfield, KY. Dr. Cal Seyfort, who announced the weather on television, kept it for him in his office. I learned from Mr. Smith that a meteor is a thing very much alive. You can't handle it with your bare hands as it will shock you or burn you. Anyway, after Dr. Seyfort met with a fatal accident some fellow stole the thing. He took it to a cave up in the mountains and made a replica of the meteor from material he got out of the cave, and placed it in the show case.

However, the fraud was soon discovered and the original was recovered and sent to the Pope, who keeps a display of meteors from all over the world. A few days ago the Pope sent Mr. Smith a letter thanking him for the meteor, and he also sent him a list of the meteorites he has, including the one from Shackle Island.

After writing the above, the telephone rang, and Mrs. Herschel Ketring of Goodlettsville called to inform me she had found an eye-witness account in her late husband's papers, of the spectacular event written by a man who was 10 years old when it happened. We expect to run his account of the meteor in next week's paper, along with other data we may accumulate in the meantime.

Now a word about that dark-haired wife of mine:

She is still in Memorial Hospital with a broken leg. Last Wednesday when I visited her I found her lying cattycornered across the bed, and I tried to move her up towards the middle. An elderly nurse came in, and I asked her to help me but she said for me to step out in the hall and she would move her. This irked me very much. Then I decided that the nurse, seeing me dressed up in my Sunday best, thought I was a preacher, and I decided to let her keep on thinking it. She finally opened the door and invited me back in, and I thanked her for moving the patient near the front. I told her I thought the patient wanted to get near the front so I could kiss her. Then I added, "But don't tell her husband about it if he happens to come in."

September 28, 1967
Gazette & Star News

Billy the Goat's Tales of Two Towns By L. D. R.

The Day Meteorites Fell At Shackle Island

As no one around Shackle Island kept a written record of the meteorite falling there the year Tennessee was 30 years old, we have to depend on an account of this spectacular event penned 70 years later by a man who was a school boy at Shackle Island at the time. He moved to West Tennessee where some 30 years elapsed before someone typed the man's account of the meteorite and sent it to kinfolks at Shackle Island.

His account as it probably appeared in a newspaper of the day is as follows:

RAIN OF METEORS

Strange Phenomenon of the Heavens just a Hundred Years Ago

Probably not many of the present generation have heard of the fall of meteors which spread apprehension over the country in 1826, a hundred years ago. The article below prepared thirty years ago by the grandfather of Mrs. J. A. Alford, tells interestingly of the phenomenon and how a church was heated because of it.

What strange things occur in this world. How the Lord furnished His church with heated stoves, of which the penman of this can and does vouch for the facts thus stated.

My memory goes back to about the year 1826—I am positive now as to the exact year. On a clear April day, about 1PM, of that year, I remember I was reciting with my class in school when my ear was startled by the loudest of reports in the heavens, which sounded like the heaviest report of cannon or thunder. It began in the West and moved East with glaring streaks of fire following in its wake. The reports were in quick succession and mingled in one continuous volley, as of one thousand heavy cannons. And it rained stones in the immediate vicinity of old Beech Church in Sumner County, Tennessee, as the result of this strange phenomenon. I have never seen anyone who could tell how or what produced this alarming spectacle. One stone fell about one hundred yards from my father's, weighing eleven pounds, sinking into the hard gravel some two feet. Other small stones fell in a straight line to one mile East of the first spoken of.

The whole community was greatly alarmed. Many thought the Day of Judgment had come. A group of field hands, negroes, among them a preacher who had been exhorting his hearers for some time but with little effect, were working together when a stone weighing seven pounds fell in their midst. The group surrounded him crying, "O, Lord, Uncle Ned, pray for us." He spurned them, saying, "Go way. I've zorted and zorted, you too late, now. Depart from me you wicked Sinners; you is took."

This strange light in the Heavens occurred the year the old stone church, Beech, was built. I can remember, though a small boy some eight or ten years old, going to Nashville with my grandfather, Rev. Hugh Kirkpatrick, Cumberland Presbyterian minister. His visit to Nashville was for the purpose of buying a pair of heating stoves for the new church. He carried the eleven pound stone with him to show to the alarmed people as the whole country was wrought up to an alarming state of mind.

I remember among the persons who examined this peculiar stone was Dr. Troost, who was collecting curiosities of the world for him museum. He was very much interested in it and proposed to purchase it, offering fifty dollars to my grandfather for it. The latter refused, saying he did not feel that he had the right to sell it, and said he had come to Nashville to purchase a pair of heating stoves for a new stone church just completed and had brought the stone along to show what had occurred.

Dr. Troost remarked, "Parson, we can now arrange that satisfactorily between us and the Lord. You give me this rock and I will give the Lord fifty dollars to furnish his house with two stoves."

And in this manner and by this strange occurrence were the first stoves of the old stone Beech church procured. It has been 70 years since I saw this curiosity from heaven, but I think I would recognize it now. It must be among the effects of Dr. Troost at Nashville. I have a desire to view it again. Will be in Nashville soon and shall look for it. H. A. Catron

It seems it's an established fact that the larger of these missiles fell on the Ketring farm at Shackle Island (spelled Catron by some) and the smaller one fell near the colored community of Mt. Olivet.

Evidently these sky visitors had a sobering influence on the citizens of these places, for there is no record of a native from either place ever being in jail. However, I recall a couple of narrow misses some of them had of becoming guests of that Gallatin Hostelry.

A native of Mt. Olivet once knocked his wife in the head with a skillet. Fortunately, Dr. Buchannan got her sewed up and, John, the anxious husband said, "Doctor, believe Hon much better."

Another time—during the depression a group of indigent farmers at Shackle Island with large families to feed went in together and formed a "corporation." They set up a moonshine still in a vacant house near a spring. One moonlight night, before they got the still in operation, they spied someone coming walking, and thought it was a revenue man, and they outran their socks getting away. As it turned out, it was one of their own gang who was late in getting there, but the scare broke up their moonshining, and gave us all something to laugh about when it leaked out.

Billy the Goat's
Tales of Two Towns
By L. D. R.

Cider making here at Vertical Plains, reminiscent of bygone days, is nearly over, but we've all enjoyed it. Although we only had half a dozen trees, they were loaded down with apples and we made about 100 gallons of cider.

First, we built a "Berlin Wall" out of barb wire and briars below the trees to keep the coons from tearing the tree down and eating them all up, and also to keep the apples from rolling down the hillside to the highway, where we would never find them.

Thanks to several of the neighbors who helped me turn the cider mill and press out the juice. They seemed to get a kick out of it, and besides, I gave them jugs of cider as well as some of the best apples we ever picked for pies. Some people in Nashville, who had never seen a cider mill in action, began coming out to help me. One young lady from the city, who was born here at Vertical Plains precisely 199 years and 11 months after the birth of George Washington, brought out her geologist husband, whose job it is to keep the State informed about the underground water resources of Tennessee. She wanted to introduce him to the above ground resources of the apple. The three of us went to the orchard and gathered a Jeep load, got them to the house by dark, then made cider by electric light after the wasps and yellow jackets had gone to roost. These pests flock to new-made cider in droves.

We made a few gallons, and I was called away, so I told the geologist he could quit. But when I returned he had ground up another

hopper full, moved it over to the press, and had squeezed out two gallons more, thereby learning for himself the art of making cider.

Two afternoons later Deba, our youngest daughter, brought two young housewives out with her from Bellshire. I already had the apples picked up and at the mill, and had figured I would have an awful time turning the mill by myself. But believe me these ladies turned that mill like Amazons, ground the cider, strained it into gallon jugs, and took all the pomace to the barn and fed it to the cows.

I gave them a gallon apiece, but they insisted, and made me take pay for it, saying they had so much fun doing something they had never seen done before. All of them, including the geologist, said they realized that the older they got, the less chance they would have of making cider again. They were right about that, because there are very few orchards in these parts now, and still fewer old fashioned cider mills.

Back a half century ago and more, every farm had an orchard, and most of them had cider mills. Back then stealing cider in the fall of the year was as much a temptation as stealing watermelons in the summer time. Mr. Green, who ran a sorghum mill at Long Hollow, also made cider. Once he had a keg of cider in his smoke house, which he kept locked. Two of his neighbors helped him kill hogs and they saw this cider keg laying back against the wall. After dark they took a brace and bit and bored a hole through the wall and on into the keg. Then they took a small rubber hose, siphoned the cider out, and drank it all up.

Uncle Will, our bachelor uncle, kept a batch on the old home place for awhile. He had plenty of apples and a cider mill. In fact, it's the same mill we made cider with the past few weeks. One year he had a keg of cider which he kept locked up in the old log smoke house. An ingenious nephew knew he kept the key on the mantle, so one cool morning he came to visit Uncle Will, who was sitting before the open fireplace reading his paper. This cunning nephew leaned upon the mantle piece, pretending he was cold, but all the while he had the key laying on a piece of paper, drawing a diagram of it with a pencil. Then he went home and made one just like it.

With this key, he and his buddies entered the door when they pleased until they had drunk up all the cider. Their old uncle didn't know where it went, when the door was always locked, and the key was still on the mantle.

It would be hypocritical to tell tales about these boys, unless I plead guilty myself, for I was a boy before they were.

Jovial "cousin" Jim Pigue had a big orchard, and kept several barrels of cider stored in his wheat garner to make vinegar. One night a big dance was held at his tenant's house, and the old joker was there, making them all laugh with his jokes and dancing with the women. Also at the dance was that infamous group of boys known as "The Board of Health" from Shackle Island. They all stood on the sidelines, because dancing was too tame for them.

Possibly to better describe their actions, it would be appropriate to repeat this stanza from the "Board's" theme song:

"Their leader said, as cousin danced a break,

There's one more raid

I'd like to make.

What might that be? they all asked him.

Said he, A raid on that cider of Uncle Jim's."

But this raid backfired on the raiders with a bang. The cider they drew to drink was out of the wrong barrel. It was hard cider, and made these cider sipping boys drunk as a "biled owl." They had to build up a fire and stay out in the woods until they sobered up. Fortunately, instead of becoming alcoholics, it broke them from ever drinking hard liquor again.

I have discovered here lately that mowing yards and getting a hair cut is all a force of habit that no one will notice, either way. A couple of Saturday evenings ago my wife called from the hospital where she still is, but doing nicely, and said for me to get a hair cut before I came to see her the next day. But I was tired as heck, and the barber shop was about ready to close so I didn't go. The next day (Sunday) I visited her, and she didn't say a word about my hair not being cut. The following Thursday I had it cut closely, and visited her again that evening, staying a couple of hours. When I got ready to leave, she said "You be sure to get a hair cut before you come back down here again."

The same applies to mowing yards. No one ever notices the difference, and I'll bet you if these yard mowers had a watermelon patch back out of sight they would spend a third less of the time chopping weeds and grass out of it than they do mowing yards. Of course, I'm an old fogy in this modern age, and spent my time working on the back side of the farm. I only show the fruits of my labor when I bring it to the house in baskets and crates, but it helps to keep from starving here at Vertical Plains.

October 19, 1967
Goodlettsville Gazette

Billy the Goat's
Tales of Two Towns
By L. D. R.

Now and then someone tells me they like to read this corny column. This I appreciate too much I guess, because it makes me wrack my feeble brain to think of something else to write.

Just the other day a prominent young businessman accosted me on the street and told me how he enjoyed it, and said his daddy always read it, too. Then he declared that his wife got a kick out of reading these wanderings of my mind. Well, thanks!

Now it has occurred to me that these two gentlemen might wonder why I, a rolling stone that gathers no moss, have never become a bigshot like them. The reason is simple: "You can get a boy out of the country, but you never can get the country out of the boy."

To begin with I never started out in life escorting the girls around. It was just the reverse with me, for when I was six years old Miss Sally, a full-grown young lady and a neighbor of ours, escorted me to school at Patton's School house on the upper reaches of Madison Creek. To keep from walking all the way around the road, we traveled a foot path across the hills and pastures of Dr. Joyner. Miss Sally kept the boogers away from me, which were mostly droves of jacks and jennets that roamed his vast holdings.

Then Miss Sally finished school and moved to Nashville and, seemingly, disappeared out of my life for I never saw her again. Eventually, I finished grade school at old St. Francis at Shackle Island, and when not in school, I worked at every kind of a job imaginable, but always in the country, such as hoeing corn,

shocking hay, tying wires at a hay baler, then stacking the hundred pound bales, sawing with a crosscut saw, splitting out hickory buggy spokes, which were in great demand back then, etc. In that manner I earned enough money to go to the nearest high school which was in Nashville.

Afterwards, I worked one whole winter with an older man hewing cross ties, which was the hardest work I ever did in my whole life. Consequently, I decided I would go to a business college and get me a job that was easier than making crossties.

How in the world my guardian angel, Miss Sally, ever learned about it I'll never know but when I got my diploma she was a stenographer for the man who owned the Maxwell House, who was also vice-president of the only $1 million bank at that time in Nashville, so she sent me word there was a job waiting for me at the American National Bank.

It was the most enjoyable and the easiest job I ever had. Each morning after we had sorted the mail, I was sent out on my route, down Market Street to other business places collecting drafts, etc. As I approached their offices, I'd hear someone say, "Here comes that damn bank clerk." It really made me feel like a big shot. Then before a year was gone, they hired a city boy to walk my route, gave me a raise, and promoted me to work on the inside. I went to work under electric lights where I couldn't feel the sun on my back or see the dogs and birds along the streets, and hear the hundreds of hoof beats of horses so similar to things in the country. So I quit the job to return to Long Hollow and the surrounding hills, which never was a bad place to live, where in clear weather both day and night, we have one of the grandest views in the whole world. Anyway you look you can see for miles and miles, but mind you, there is only one way you can possibly look, and that is straight up over your head.

No, they didn't fire me, in fact, two of the upper echelon dignitaries talked to me for an hour trying to persuade me to stay, because they knew I always obeyed orders given me, although by so doing, one of their best customers, who gave me a good cussing, was lost. I had refused to accept a check from a prominent wool and ginseng dealer unless it was certified. The man really cussed me out until I told him I wasn't the president of the bank—only an errand boy.

When I arrived back at the bank and assistant cashier called me on the carpet for what I had done, and told me this firm had transferred their business to another bank after I left. Well, I came out of the scrape with flying colors. Later, the assistant sheepishly told me that the cashier, who was an old bachelor who rode horseback to work, had given the order not to accept a check unless it was certified that morning and he hadn't known about it.

Then there was the time I was handed $800 to wrap and seal with sealing wax and put on the train for Monterey minutes before the train was due to leave. I called for a boy to go with me, according to the insurance company's orders. Telling the boy we would have to run every foot of the way, we lit out down the center of Market Street. The boy gave out and sat down on the curb, but I kept going. When I got in sight of the depot the train was leaving and the gatekeeper tried to stop me, but I dodged him and overtook the Tennessee Central. I threw the money into the express car, then picked up my receipt book further up the track after it was signed and thrown out.

October 26, 1967
Goodlettsville Gazette

Billy the Goat's Tales of Two Towns By L. D. R.

The greatest scourge to becoming old is to have a half a dozen older friends you like to visit and enjoy talking to, then have one of them called from the scene of action here on Earth. This is the predicament I am in today. Consequently, I don't feel in the mood to write a hilarious joke column, but am constrained to eulogize this great and good friend of mine, who put Shackle Island on the map by becoming one of the most trusted medical doctors in this part of the state.

This man has been a guiding spirit in my whole life. When I applied for my first important job, his name was given for a reference. That I and the bunch I grew up with were as wild as bucks, he must have seen enough good underneath to give me a favorable recommendation, for I got the job.

Then when I started dating a girl whom I knew absolutely nothing about, but who had waited on a sick lady patient of his, he voluntarily told me that she was a fine young lady. So we always felt elated that the mother of the children of Vertical Plains came well recommended. When the nine children were born, he was the good Samaritan who ushered them into this old world and cared for them through all their childhood sicknesses. He used to laugh and say that they were all born in the same house in the same corner of the room. Perhaps he was right, I don't remember.

Some of the six oldest children had seven or more cases of pneumonia, and he came twice a day to see them when they were at their worst. One little boy had pneumonia the third time, and the doctor almost despaired

of him, and gave orders one afternoon that the boy be given a spoonful of a strong liquid every hour during the night. But the boy refused to take it, saying his mother had told him the stuff would kill him.

Thanks though to Billie Blue, a good neighbor who sat up with him that night, he revived. Billie gave him a quarter every time he took a spoonful and the next morning the boy was much better and had a handful of money. He never made a drunkard.

One little girl who had Bright's disease was also bad off with pneumonia, but the doctor did what skeptics said was impossible: He cured her when he called a wholesale druggist in Nashville and had him open up on a Sunday morning and let me have the latest medicine out. She is hale and hearty today, and the mother of two sons.

More than once I've heard this genial doctor laugh and tell this story: He was called in a hurry one night to see Aunt Hale, a widow woman who was having spasm with cramp colic. He quickly reached for his hypodermic needle and began rolling up her sleeve, when she yelled, "It's not my arm that hurts, doctor! It's my belly!"

Now a word about the greatest tranquilizers which he and I and others sometimes have had to rely on—a chew of tobacco. His older brother, a young minister chewed it and it saved his life once. The doctor and his brother lived on a farm near Murfreesboro while their daddy was Governor of Tennessee. The boys looked after the farm. On it they had a big corn crib, built a couple of feet off the ground, with sheds all around. One time a big old sow farrowed a litter of pigs under it. The young preacher crawled up under the crib to count the pigs, and here came the angry old sow, a booing and her mouth wide open. He had nothing to defend himself, but just as she was ready to clamp down with that open mouth to chew up his face, he let go a mouth full of tobacco juice, and hit the old critter right in the eye. She squealed in pain, and ran out into the barn lot, then the young fellow counted the pigs.

The doctor was always ready to render me a friendly deed, but when he first started practicing at Shackle Island I, a teenage boy, was one of the first to do a drastic act to benefit him. His buggy horse would scare every time he drove by a newly installed chicken roost built beside the road, and we boys dumped it into the creek. Thus began a legend. The owner threatened every boy in the neighborhood who was innocent (and some of us who were guilty) with the law. Then she received a letter signed, "The Shackle Island Board of Health." It read in part like this: "We regret very much that we have aroused your displeasure, but beg to inform you that the health and safety of every wayfarer who passes along the highway demanded that the structure be removed, making it imperative that we do our duty." Evidently this splendid lady forgave us for our audacity, when the boy who strained the hardest and laughed the loudest in that moving episode, a few years later became her son-in-law.

I haven't told in this corny column who this doctor was, but now I'll do it by quoting his son, himself a popular doctor,—a statement that impressed me very much as we stood in the home beside the casket, "He was a good one."

May 16, 1968
Goodlettsville Gazette

Billy the Goat's Tales of Two Towns By L.D.R.

Some things are possible and some are impossible. Back in the days when wagons and teams were the only local modes of transportation, I used to hear fellows sing out, "Popped whip and hollered 'haw,' and I heard my voice in Arkansas." Then they changed to "Popped my whip and hollered 'gee' and I heard my voice in Tennessee." Come to think of it, that would have been impossible unless he drove his team up the middle of the Mississippi River, which would had to have been bone dry at the time.

But last Saturday I unwittingly popped off my mouth, and although I won't hear it there myself, people in Germany will hear it soon regardless of what impression it makes on the people there. Some there I know already read this column. The way this happened is like this:

General Eiselar and his wife from Wermheim, Germany were visiting daughter Deba and her family, and they brought their guests out to Vertical Plains to visit us and several of our children who had gathered here. She boarded with them for awhile during her stay in Germany when her husband was in service. They asked Mina to play the piano, so the upset of it all was our three youngest children and their husbands put on a "Grand Ole Opry" right here in our front room. The six of them sang all of the old songs of yesteryear, accompanied by the piano and guitar played by Deba.

The General and his wife were very sociable and smiling people and they seemed to enjoy the musical program very much.

Then these two gathered right in front of me and began asking questions of how long we had lived at Vertical Plains, and I told them quite a bit of our life's history—told them a joke or two then sang the famous hobo song of three score years ago vintage for them. Well, to my astonishment the lady switched a button on a little contraption not much bigger than a billfold, and it repeated my every word, including the song. So I was bugged right in my own home. They also made records of all the songs the children sang for them to carry back to Germany to play for their friends there.

These visitors left Deba's home Sunday afternoon, and Tommy, her husband, said that they had that little gadget turned on full blast and my voice was what he heard plainly singing that old song, which winds up "He went down the railroad track, waiting for the train to come back. Along came the little Dixie Flyer, away behind time. He jumped at the cowcatcher and caught the blind. Oh, he is long-g-g-gone."

In their nephew's little terrapin car they had borrowed when they arrived in America, this couple left for Huntsville, Alabama to spend a week with that great German scientist, Werner Von Braun.

Speaking of scientists, the other day a science teacher passed the greatest compliment about me that could ever be passed on a man in this modern age, and I'm duly proud of it. On being told that never in my life had I ever run a lawn mower, he said it was the most outstanding thing he ever heard of that I had never tried to keep up with the Joneses like other men do. The fact is I've never had a reason for mowing the yard, because the powers that be in this habitat of "Do this and don't do that" have always insisted that I keep the chickens stopped out of the yard, so with no hens' nests to find, why worry mowing the grass down?

I recall that when a boy, I used to mow down the high weeds in the yard with an old crooked handle mowing blade to find a goose's nest or a guinea's nest. One year an old burdock grew up around the barn, and I found a guinea's nest with 81 eggs in it. So nobody can ever say I haven't mowed yards when there was a reason to mow, but those days are gone and are just memories in the past. Even the radio has quit singing "Old McDonald had a farm" to remind us of life in the past out on the farm.

However, there is one great pleasure still remaining here on the farm—strawberries are ripe, raspberries are in full bloom. So from now on this summer I may be too busy picking berries to write this column.

Anyway, one reader tells me to write something about George Wallace, but I know nothing to write about him. However, everyone around Shackle Island is for him tooth and toenail, and one prominent fellow says that Wallace is the only candidate in the race who can take care of this country, the mess it is in today.

June 13, 1968
Goodlettsville Gazette

Billy the Goat's Tales of Two Towns By L.D.R.

This season of the year is when dog days start here at Vertical Plains. Already a whole car load of our offspring has started vacationing. They left Monday morning to visit Mrs. Steve Boyd, our married granddaughter in Blowing Rock, N. C. That morning they brought Old Scratcher, one of their dogs, for me to feed and watch after while they are gone. Their other dog, a pedigreed Dutch hound, they carried to a kennel on Dickerson Road where they pay $1.50 day for his keep. Maybe they don't know it, but I'm getting a thousand and fifty cents every day I keep Old Scratcher, for that dog has the worst case of halitosis a dog can possibly have, because he had little enough sense to tackle a pole cat the night before they brought him to me.

Now that so many people are being assassinated and so many banks are being held up, the gun lobbyists won't hear to them stopping the sale and manufacture of guns. I'm in favor of doing away completely with guns that are fired with gunpowder. Look at China. They were the first to invent gunpowder, and what a fix they are in today! So why not have all guns made to fire tear gas only, and that made from pole cat venom? Had they had a Matt Dillon in Los Angeles the other night to fire pole cat's venom into the assassin's eyes, no other shot would have been fired.

Maybe you think we can't do without firearms today, but the Indians and Robin Hood got by with only bows and arrows, which are weapons that can't easily be concealed. Further more, before their day, David slew a giant with his sling shot, so why

not let's revert back to these old time weapons that are not nearly so dangerous?

Anyway, in this gun control effort, they are starting at the top of the ladder and coming down. Years ago they should have stopped the sale of toy pistols to the parents of every boy in the whole country, because it encouraged boys when they grew up to want a real pistol, which was against the law for them to carry.

On the other hand, girls have always been given dolls to make them love children and have patience with the, which was seemingly a good thing. But today there is a great hue and cry about the population explosion all over the world. Maybe they should have been given rocking horses so they would have made "tomboys" who didn't give a hoot about children.

Maybe law officers will be compelled to carry fire arms as long as it is possible for criminals to get hold of them, but the only man who was ever elected sheriff for Sumner County from the 6th District carried a gun, but never used it. All the law breakers around Gallatin knew he wouldn't, so they would try to outrun him, but he always caught them. The jailbirds nicknamed him "Old Big Foot," because he could outrun them in a foot race. Once he jumped off his horse and ran a fellow a mile across fields and fences before catching him or knowing who he was or what he was running for, then found the man was wanted in Kentucky for something.

Here is something that may help some of you readers with your gardens: last year the crows pulled up all of four rows of corn to get the grain it sprouted from. This year, before I planted the garden I heard crows "cawing" at the far end every morning before I got out of bed. They were looking where I had disked to see if anything had come up. Where I had dug up some squash plants and set them out in a row next to the fence, the crows pulled up a number of them to see if there was a grain of corn underneath. When I planted the corn and beans there this year, I didn't try to shoot the crows, because they are so wary it would have been almost impossible. Before anything came up I criss-crossed the garden with bailer twine, running from fence to fence, then put up a scare crow. However, what I think trumped the crows more than anything was several green water hoses that I strung out along the rows that looked so much like snakes I even jumped away from them a time or two, myself.

The upset of all this is the corn has been up a whole week, and growing vigorously, and not a stalk has been pulled up nor has a crow been heard near the garden.

August 22, 1968
Goodlettsville Gazette

Billy the Goat's Tales of Two Towns By L. D. R.

Although we had gotten a good rain and the weather had moderated, Sunday was a lonesome day here at Vertical Plains. All the children living nearby were busy watching ball games on TV or attending church services. But we did have an enjoyable chat with Mr. and Mrs. Irvin Gourley, when they drove by for a short visit. I was glad indeed to meet Mrs. Gourley, who confirmed the truth of an old story by saying she had heard all her life about an amusing drama that I, too, had heard all my life.

The participants in it were her great grandfather, Squire Alex Honeycutt, and my own grandfather Squire W. B. Gilliam, who both served as magistrates in the Sassafras District of Sumner County. Squire Alex was also a Baptist preacher, and Squire Gilliam was also a singing master. He was teaching singing where the preacher's son was a student. Every time Grandpa Gilliam sounded his tuning fork for the class to get the tune, and they started singing, Squire Alex would interrupt by shouting, "Hold on, Mr. Gilliam! Brat ain't got the sound yet."

Afterwards, Grandpa moved to Long Hollow and told his story often until it got to be a byword and many times when I was a boy and staying at his house, in the dead hours of night, I've heard people drive by and awaken us all by yelling, "Hold on, Mr. Gilliam! Brat ain't got the sound yet!"

Later that Sunday afternoon, LD Jr. and daughter, Sharon, broke the monotony of the day by taking his mother and me out "buggy riding" in their new car. Over on Center Point Road we drove in the driveway and stopped at the home of Mr. and Mrs. Charlie Rice, the veteran rabbit hunter. Charlie's wife was able to walk out to the car and talk with Mrs. Hester. I consider Charlie one of my best friends, but I have to fuss with him sometimes for calling me "Mr. Luther," making folks think I am older than he is, when the truth of the matter is on that November day long ago when I was born, the hunting season was open and rabbits were running scared, like as if Charlie were after them and really he was about old enough to crawl out of his cradle and take after them.

Now here is a story I want you to read about the fidelity and concern of a mother's love. Some of our children live far away, and if their mother doesn't get a letter from them once a week she is terribly upset. Last Wednesday our daughter Onezima (Mrs. Lawrence Bradley) came and carried her mother to Vanderbilt for a therapy treatment. I went to Nashville in a truck to take the big Angus bull to sell, to stop him from roaming over the neighborhood, but I got back before they did and brought the mail in.

There was a letter in the mail from Juanita in Edmond, Oklahoma, which I opened and read, and then gave to Mrs. Hester when she returned home. Then about supper time, she told me she had also found one from Jimmie T., our son in Sacramento, that had been opened, too, and that I could get it and read it, then put back in the dresser where the rest could read it.

I found the letter to be quite interesting. In it he told about the problems his wife, Mary, who is a registered nurse, had as superintendent of the big new hospital at Davis, California, which they have just acquired. Then he mentioned how their three daughters were doing in school. He also commended President Johnson for declaring he wouldn't seek re-election, avoiding becoming a target for the doves that are seeking office.

Then he stated that he hadn't decided yet whether or not he would again teach in the Sacramento City College this fall. Next, of all things, he gave me honorable mention in his letter by saying, "Tell Daddy to keep the paths up and down the hills well trod, for I am sure it does him a lot of good!" Now all of this has interested you one bit, but I know it certainly helped this boy's mother, because she got up the next morning and had breakfast on the table before I woke up. That was the first time all the summer she has done that without me assisting her to walk and move about. Maybe it's pure devilment in me, but I got a big laugh out of that letter, for it was dated April 8th! Four months later she had pulled an April Fool on herself by picking up and reading an old letter without noticing the date! The absent-minded professor is always the one that makes such mistakes. This lady's youngest daughter, who for 10 years was a teller in the Bank of Goodlettsville, read the letter and failed to see the joke until she was shown the date on the letter. We haven't shown her mother the date yet because some things she doesn't know does her more good that what she does know. Perhaps she may not like hearing about it in this column.

Anyway, it doesn't make too much difference, because although she won't admit it, she has always thought too much of me. Like many other mothers, she named our first son after me and Uncle Sam has been confused ever since, and now the State of Tennessee is confused, too. Yesterday a state inspector stopped at the wrong mail box like the mail does. When he finally arrived at Vertical Plains I told Mrs. Hester I was going with him to the berry patch, and she asked what his name was. I told her I didn't know. Then, still showing concern for me, she forbid me to go up there through the woods with someone I didn't know.

However, I went anyway and found the fellow to be perfectly safe to be with in the woods. He takes this paper and reads the column. Now that this inspector has okayed the red raspberry plants, we plan to dig them in November and sell them.

October 17, 1968
Goodlettsville Gazette

Billy the Goat's Tales of Two Towns By L. D. R.

Although it rained all day Sunday, October 6, there was a great turnout at Peay Memorial Park in Goodlettsville for the first reunion of Ralphs, who originated in Long Hollow. Present were the fourth generation, along with the fifth and sixth and a small sprinkling of the seventh.

Strange as it may sound, the first three generations of Ralphs never existed until the fourth became of age, because up until then their name was pronounced "Rafe," but we younger ones rebelled against this and began calling our names what it actually spelled.

Louis Ralph and wife, Polly, moved into Long Hollow in the early part of the 19th century, from where, no one knew, because they didn't think to keep a record or, at least, we have no record. Several of their children migrated west before the Civil War and one disappeared in that war, while one son named Tyree was a home body and settled down at the old home place where his sons and daughters were born to him and his wife, Sarah McMurtry. All of them were honest, hard working people with varied personalities. Some were talkers and others great eaters, while the eldest was a great saver. He trimmed all their meat for them, and when they sold backbones and spare ribs, that was exactly what they sold, according to the old time merchants. They declared all the meat had been sand papered off the bones. Maybe it had. Uncle Will knew what made the best sausage.

Another of these uncles liked to eat so well it made him poor. One day he went to the Nashville market and forgot to carry along a satchel full of grub, so he went to a sandwich stand and ate 12 big hamburgers. Then he told the manager they should be cheaper by the dozen, and by speaking up, got his coffee free.

Now a word about this talking uncle, who, although he never went to school but a week of two in his life, could talk to anyone he met. One morning two women accompanied by two small children, stopped at a store in Goodlettsville, and as they walked out, one of the women dropped a watermelon she had picked up and had hidden under her apron and it burst wide open.

The merchant had them arrested and they were told to sit out on the side of the street until 4:00 o'clock that afternoon, when the magistrate would return home on the train to hold court and try them. All the other merchants up and down the street were very indignant about these poor people being kept out in the sun all day, but all were afraid to say a word about it to this merchant, who didn't allow them to meddle with his affairs.

About Noon Uncle Frank showed up in town and they detailed him to do the talking. "Er-rah! I hear you got some of our Shackle Island folks arrested," he said. "I'm here to settle this thing. Here is a quarter for your watermelon, and I'm bringing them in to tell you they're sorry. Then we're turning them loose and letting them go back home." So that's all there was to it. The merchant, a life-long friend of this self-styled "judge and jury" didn't try to out-talk him.

In all there were 150 Ralph descendants and their husbands and wives who braved the rain and missed the World Series to attend this reunion. It would be impossible to name them all in this column for lack of space. However, this writer was the oldest one there, and the oldest one living today. The sponsors of this get-together, and to whom we are all indebted, were Deba and George.

Deba is our youngest daughter and George is the oldest in-law. Recently Deba recalled how she and her sister, when they were little tots, were taught not to fight. She told that "Daddy rubbed their heads together," and I was surprised that she still remembers it. Anyway, they are two of the most peaceful sisters who ever lived. On the other hand George can tell you how he learned not to talk too much. He was very finicky about whose cooking he ate. When he and my sister Lura first married they visited Uncle Buck, a sweet potato grower who always presented all his guests with a big juicy baked sweet potato. Uncle Buck offered George one, he declined to accept it, telling the old gentleman that he never ate them except when he was at the table where he could wash it down with a glass of buttermilk, and that's when he talked too much. For immediately Uncle Buck brought him a big glass of buttermilk—the very thing he didn't like to drink away from home—and he had to sit there and choke that potato and milk down to keep from offending his host. So Deba and George both learned their lessons well, and were well qualified to be the sponsors of this reunion.

January 16, 1969
Goodlettsville Gazette

Billy the Goat's Tales of Two Towns By L. D. R.

This New Year came in like a lion, and so far it has been cold and blustery with snow on the ground. However, Shackle Islanders seldom worry about the weather. They think of the legendary Dick Hullett and his optimistic attitude towards the weather conditions.

The story goes, and has been told many times, that in '88 there came the biggest snow on record in these parts which stayed on the ground a couple of weeks, making it impossible for people to get out to work to make a living. A benevolent farmer, who Dick worked for some times, filled a big wheat sack with provisions from his smoke house and cellar and carried them to Dick's house. When the farmer carried the sack of grub in, he found this optimistic old timer sitting in front of the fire with his family parching corn to eat, and exclaimed, "You old rascal, I knew you wouldn't have a thing to eat but parched corn," and Dick answered, "There's many a one that ain't got that much to eat."

There have been dozens of stories told about this shrewd old fellow, who always seemed to have luck on his side. Here is the latest one, which I heard only last week:

A man at Shackle Island bet Dick five dollars he would beat him in a horse race across a corn field to the fence on the other side. This crafty old fellow told the man he didn't own a horse, but if he would let him ride behind him on the horse he was riding he would take the bet. The horseman accepted the bet, thinking he had some easy money made, then started the horse galloping across

the field with Dick on behind, holding tight to the back of the saddle.

As they neared the fence the rider in the saddle started to reach out to touch the fence, and at the same instant Dick touched the horse in the flanks, with both heels, causing the animal to buck and throw him over the other fellow's head, landing him astraddle the top rail of the fence to win the five dollar bet.

About 60 years ago two other boys and I were attending school in Nashville and boarding on 8th Avenue, just below the old Custom House. We were boarding with my great aunt and her daughter, who ran the boarding house. One Sunday afternoon a novelty salesman from New York City breezed in and rented a room for a week. He was a noisy young fellow, who took in the town until nearly midnight, then came blustering in and up the stairway to his room, singing or yelling like a wildcat, awakening the whole household. We never held that against him, but just thought that was the way he was raised. One cold morning about the middle of the week he found himself in the front room downstairs by a nice, warm fire in the grate. We boys had gone to school, and the others had gone to work. While all alone he really showed his raising by heating the poker red hot and burning his full name on the white enamel hearth in boxcar letters.

Cousin Mina, the landlady, was terribly angry when she discovered what he had done. After he had left for uptown, she declared she would make him leave that very night, but for the fact his rent was paid up until the end of the week. "Well, he is leaving tonight anyway, when he discovers this house is haunted," I told her, and she didn't say anything.

A nickel lump of rosin was bought and a black spool of thread was borrowed. The salesman's room was at the far end of the hall, two doors from the room we boys occupied. Luckily, there were transoms over all the doors, and the ancient walnut bed he slept on had a thin panel in the headboard, and was just inside the door of his room. The thread we fastened with a stout pin to the backside of the thin panel, and pulled the thread out over the transom and on to our room.

Some time after 11:00 o'clock he came up the stairs as noisy as ever, and we let him turn out the light and go to bed. Then we opened our door slightly and began rubbing the thread with the chunk of rosin. It made no noise where we were, but it made the head of his bed sound like a dozen buzz saws were tearing it to pieces.

His feet hit the floor with a thump, and he turned on his light, then finally he came out in the hall and searched the bath room. Then he came to our door yelling to awaken us, and trying to open the door, which we were all braced against with the light out. Eventually, he returned to his room, turned off his light and went back to bed. But as soon as he did that, the headboard began again to wail and shriek like a banshee. He must have thought the devil was after him, because as the clock struck 12, he was going down the stairway, his suit case in his hands, and that was the last we ever saw or heard tell him.

Note: a non-violent way of getting rid of an unwanted nuisance.

April 24, 1969
Goodlettsville Gazette

Billy the Goat's Tales of Two Towns By L. D. R.

Reading the papers today about all the strife and turmoil in this country makes an old timer grateful that he was ten years old when this century began. Back then we went to school to learn and let our teachers run the schools, Later we got a job and worked for a lot less pay than people do today. Still we never thought of striking for higher wages, and we always tried to do everything we were physically and mentally able to do that our boss told us.

My memories go back to a small boy helping on a rough hill farm and garden to eke out an existence for the family and livestock, grubbing bushes and hoeing corn for other farmers and building chicken coops for their wives, to earn spending money.

Later, becoming a jack of all trades, first tying wires on 200 heavy bales of hay each day, then stacking them around an old-fashioned hay baler for $1.25 per day. Then I remember making cross ties all winter to make money to go to high school and business college. All these are pleasant memories, and many more, besides they all occurred in the open spaces of the country.

Then to the city to work, where the hardest job I ever did in my whole life I did with my tongue, when I refused to accept a check without its being certified. It was a big business house on Market Street where they had always treated me so nice when I had made previous collections. But this time they cussed me black and blue until I assured them I was the lowest employee at the bank and I had to do it to hold my job.

The next genuine cussing I got was when a teller at the bank waited until almost train time to hand me $800 to wrap and seal and then get on the train for Monterey. I ran every foot of the way to the depot out in the middle of the street, then dodged under the gatekeeper's arm, who was holding it half open demanding my ticket. The train was already moving away, and I outran it until I reached the express car. The door was open, and I threw the money in the car and also the express book for the man, whose feet I threw it at, to sign, then slowly walked on beside the tracks until I found the book he had signed and thrown out. Walking back by the depot out they came and began bawling me out. I laughed at them and told them I was ordered to get the money on the train, and I had my receipt for it there in my hand.

I was promoted at the bank to a job that kept me inside all the time, and the fun was over on the street then. I quit, although two officials pleaded with me for an hour to stay on. I've never regretted my action, for then I went west, where no one ever cussed me again, because I was from Tennessee. People out there believed a Tennessean would shoot them if he were ever antagonized. Of course, there was nothing to such a belief, but as long as they believed it, it worked wonders.

An employment agent once sent me out to work on a farm, as they called it, but I traveled over 60 miles on a train and never saw a farm. I then traveled several miles further in a two-horse wagon that stopped in a deep canyon with a river running through it. I arrived there one Sunday at noon, and they put me to work that afternoon, reconstructing a washed out irrigation reservoir. They gave me a pick and shovel and put me down in a muddy place to loosen up the dirt and mud so they could haul it out with old-fashioned horse drawn scrapers or dirt haulers. I had to hold these scrapers down by the two handles while the team pulled it through bog to get a load. That alone was much of a man's job. All that afternoon and all the next day, Mr. Hardy, the civil engineer, sat on the bank and instructed me what to do and how, never finding any fault with me or hurrying me. However, he had a big black-bearded straw boss who was working further down the river with the rest of the gang.

Both nights in the tents where we ate and slept, I heard the men telling how mean this straw boss was, and how they would like to kill him. Tuesday morning Mr. Hardy stayed in his office and soon after I started work along came the straw boss and yelled, "Do about down there, Slim," which made me mad as a hornet. An hour later he returned and yelled, "You'll have to let that shovel work a little faster!"

I threw my shovel backward over my head, then answered, "Darned, if I have to do anything! If you don't like my work give me my time." I was facing him with my hands swinging near my pockets. He evidently thought I was going to shoot him, for he quickly turned and walked away, saying, "See Mr. Hardy if you want to quit," which I promptly did. In the tent I overheard the cook and his helper laughing about how I had bluffed the hated bully, and wondering if I were another Billy the Kid. Bluff it was, too, for I never carried a pistol in my life.

May 1, 1969
Goodlettsville Gazette

Billy the Goat's Tales of Two Towns By L. D. R.

In today's automobile age there is nothing happening that is humorous enough to report, so we will have to revert back to the transition period between horse and buggy and the automobile to find something worth telling.

One of the oldest stories on record about this change in modes of traveling concerns the old farmer who lived so far back in the hills he had never heard of a gas propelled vehicle. One day he ventured out on a highway and he met an automobile followed by a motorcycle, and his horse ran away with the buggy. When some men working along the road stopped his horse and asked what caused him to run away, the old fellow answered, "I met a four wheel thing getting its breath awfully loud, because there was no horse pulling it, and I could hardly hold my horse, and then along came a colt following it, and popping like a pack of firecrackers. That scared the old rascal so bad he ran away with me."

One of my own uncles had a buggy horse that was old enough to vote in a horse election when autos first invaded the highways. Every time he would see a car coming he would turn the horse off the road, get his head against a fence, then jump out and hold a big feed bag over the horse's head until the monster drove by. It was hard to tell which was the scaredest, the man or the horse.

I remember well my first ride in an automobile. A group of us boys from Shackle Island were staying in town going to school. One of them, however, wasn't going to school but was chauffeuring for a rich business man there. One night he brought the car to the boarding house to take us boys for a ride. We drove out Harding Road at a moderate speed. At one place he remarked, "You boys remember this spot when we come back over it." I didn't think I would remember it on a dark night like that, but I did, and still do, for when we neared the spot coming back, he pulled the throttle down, and the car sped over a bump, throwing the three of us in the back seat up and bumping our heads on the steel frame of the roof.

When the city people first began driving their cars out over our country roads they didn't travel much faster than a horse and buggy, and they always bowed and spoke to us country hunks when they met us on the road. Soon afterwards they began shipping second hand T Model Fords from the North down here, and most every boy in the country bought one, then began driving them to see how fast they would go. Soon the women folks caught that dreadful disease called speed. Today on this crooked Long Hollow Pike, where there is no speed limit, everybody, with the exception of a few old timers, drives through here like rocket ships to the moon.

Back to the Model T days—one young fellow who grew up at Shackle Island on a rough hill farm moved to Nashville with his folks and got a job where he made enough money to buy a second hand Model T. Then he got in the thing and drove it out to Goodlettsville. There he visited with some friends, and after parading up and down the streets awhile, he headed for Shackle Island, his old stomping grounds. As he came down by the old rock bank, he was driving so fast he couldn't make the turn out Long Hollow Pike, and, consequently, he knocked down a yard fence and stopped his car on the front porch of the house on the corner. He eventually made it on to Shackle Island. His trip back home proved quite a historical coincidence, for it was the Fourth of July, the day we celebrate as commemorating the signing of the Declaration of Independence. As all of you know, the first man to sign this famous document was John Hancock, and the bearded old gentleman who lived in the house where the fence was knocked down and the car stopped on the front porch was named John Hancock.

The other fellow is not the only one the joke is on concerning these ancient cars. The first car we ever owned was an old T Model we paid $80 for, plus $10 for another radiator, after a grocery truck on First Street darted past me, then stopped in front of a store, directly in front of me, the first time I drove the thing to Nashville.

We have an encouraging report about Mrs. Hester, the queen of Vertical Plains for the last 52 years, who has been in Vanderbilt Hospital the past two weeks taking that new medicine for Parkinson's Disease. We all, including the nurses, think she is getting much better. Her doctor wants her to stay there at least three weeks, then continue taking the medicine at home.

However, I am saddened writing the column this week, because two of its esteemed readers recently passed away. They were both splendid gentlemen and both encouraged me in writing this haphazard column. The fact that so many say they like to read it is a great satisfaction to me.

July 24, 1969
Goodlettsville Gazette

Billy the Goat's
Tales of Two Towns
By L. D. R.

Much has been said and written about Country Music and all day singing, but few people these days ever hear any real country music. They stay inside all day, with the doors closed, and shiver through the hot days, missing the most of living.

Being one who stays out in the fields all day or under the shade of the trees in the yard, far away from the artificial frosts of living, it is easy to hear and enjoy the serenades of Mother Nature. Some of it is very pleasing and some of it very irritating, but none more so than that we hear on the TV machine.

All this melody starts at daybreak with the mockingbirds singing in the old thorn tree where they have their nest. When the Sun comes up the Roberts tribes come on the air to stay until sundown and let no one go to sleep on the job, but what their shrill call of "Bob White" will awaken. If there are roasting ears getting ripe, the "cawing" of the crows at dawn is a warning to get to the garden in a hurry and stretch some baler twine tied together across the rows. If you don't do this the crows will eat the corn up and leave you nothing but the shucks.

This dry, hot weather, when there are no clouds in the sky, the July flies sing all day. They are better known as old dry flies because they decry dry weather. What we are hoping for now is the "kook kook" of the rain crow predicting rain to come soon. Every night when the Sun goes down the katydids take over in the tree tops with their ear splitting noise. This racket first started this year on the 7th of July, which means we will have our first frost the seventh of October, three months from now.

Katydids are the most sensitive of all creatures. No matter how big the tree is in which he is singing, if you place your hand on the tree he will stop his song. If you don't understand why the pronoun "he" was used, the "women folks" in his family have no voice whatever, we are told. Now wouldn't it be awful if the human family was like katydids? At least this column would get very little encouragement for only a few men admit reading it. Thanks to the many ladies who comment about it and make it worthwhile to write it when there is really nothing worthwhile to write.

The drummer boy of this wild outdoor band is on his summer vacation now because there are so many insects crawling around everywhere he doesn't have to drum for a living. Red Woodpecker will be back on the job this winter drumming on old fence rails or gate posts to find a worm for his breakfast.

The most discordant note of all comes from Old Whistler, the ground hog, who is eating up our garden. Even in the Spring before the gardens were planted we witnessed his shadow, a high powered H.L.K. rifle following him around. Now since the weather has gotten hot and our gardens are flourishing, that expert seeing eye that looked down the barrel of that rifle has quit coming around. When you read this please tell him that the old rascal is eating up our tomato vines before they ever bloom. It won't necessarily have to be that brand of rifle, it could be a J.H.J or S, if John Henry Jones or Smith owns one and can draw a bead on the scavenger and save our garden.

These named melodies are just a few that have been with us on the farm down through the ages, but there were many more we will never be able to hear again. For instance, we used to hear hens "a cackling" and roosters crowing on every farm. Then the automobiles appeared and made it unsafe to raise chickens near the highway. In the old days there were cow bells ringing on every hill and in every valley, now for the same reason they are all fenced in and don't need to be hunted at night. We never hear some country fellow yodeling in the distance at night. These days they are either gone to a show or are at home listening to someone else yodel over the air.

Living in the past? Yes, as I have been accused of many times, so here is a quip more up to date and more appetizing. The other day we drove up to the Paul Owen orchard and I soon found myself to be "Owen" Paul—for a basket of peaches.

July 31, 1969
Goodlettsville Gazette

Billy the Goat's Tales of Two Towns By L. D. R.

This column is being written in the form of a letter to my grandsons in California and elsewhere because their Granddaddy spent time in the West more than half a century ago.

So boys, let me state that long before I ever left home I had learned there was one golden rule to go by: "Render unto Caesar the things that are Caesar's." I hope you understand, boys, that Caesar is your employer—the man who pays your salary. If he tells you to report for work at a certain time, be sure that your boss is always able to bet ten to one that you report for work on time.

When I stepped off the train in that wild and wooly country in 1912, I already had a job with the richest concern in all of the West. They owned mines, railroads and had absolute control of the latest frontier town in the Rockies, as well as owning and operating the biggest department store in the West. Here in this big store they put me to work as a clerk in the Banking Department because I had experience in that line of work. When I had worked about two weeks the president of the company picked me out of all his 200 employees to send me to this newly built frontier town in the mountains to help the manager run the store. However, some of my friends, who migrated there from Shackle Island years before and had become managers in this big store, advised me not to take this job up in the mountains, saying nobody could get along with the manager of that store. He had been sent up there to run it to get rid of

him at the big store, since no one could get along with him.

Thank goodness, though, I had chosen to render unto Caesar (the president of the whole layout) and accepted the job, feeling confident I could get along with anyone by using the same golden rule. I worked amiably with this new boss, because I did what he told me to do, and never made any complaint. One day, for instance my new boss sold a half ton of baled hay to a townsman who owned a cow, and told me to deliver it to the man's tent a half mile away. At the time trucks hadn't been invented, and there wasn't any delivery wagon in the whole town, so I hitched up myself to a two-wheel cart that we used to transfer merchandise from the warehouse to the store, and that old cow didn't go hungry that night.

In this little town, they had a school house, which was used for school during the week, for preaching services on Sunday, and one night during the week for dancing. One night my boss declared we would close the store early and go to the dance.

We were standing watching the dance when my boss told me to get in the ring and dance with them. I told him I had never learned to dance, but Mr. Kelley, a grey haired Irishman, who was superintendent of the town, was standing by. He told his wife to dance with me. I had often waited on this grey-haired lady in the store, so she agreed with a smile to teach me how to dance. It was one of those swinging dances, and she gave all the rest of the women a wink, causing each one of them to swing me around several times extra. That dance lasted an eternity, and when it stopped I staggered to the wall as drunk as a "biled owl!" They got a big laugh out of me, but I had rendered unto the two big Caesars over me and proved I was no tenderfoot.

Physical performances like this probably made no impression on this boss, who all my friends thought would be impossible to work under. But head work did the trick, as you are supposed to rely on some time.

The first week I worked in this store a Mexican youth about grown who couldn't speak of word of English came in the store with money in his hand and asked for something. It took my boss an hour or two to find someone to interpret what he was asking for. As it turned out he wanted a stamped envelope from the Post Office in the store, causing me to see the need to learning the Mexican language. That evening after the boss went home and left me to close the store after all the loafers left, I found an excellent teacher, and began learning this language. I soon learned what most everything in the store was called by this foreign language gang of railroad workers, and also what they called our money, as well as how to thank them for it when they paid me, which pleased these fellows very much.

Pretty soon my boss noticed me talking this jargon to the Mexicans, and how they responded to it, and declared his amazement that I had learned so quickly, when he had been there six months and couldn't understand a word they spoke. He then detailed me to wait on these fellows every time one came in, but I never did tell him that my special friend, Ralph Gonzales, a Mexican, was teaching me every night when he loafed in the store.

When word came from the main store to lay me off until the weather opened up in the Spring, this hard boiled little Yankee (Caesar who I had rendered unto in many ways without losing my dignity) thought I was one of the seven wonders of the West, and made me promise to come back to work when he called me. But I soon met another Caesar to render unto, and never went back.

September 24, 1970
Goodlettsville Gazette

Billy the Goat's
Tales of Two Towns
By L. D. R.

Ever since he and his delightful family visited us here two years ago, I've been getting messages from my rancher friend in Texas wanting me to write him a long letter. He and I grew up together at Shackle Island. He, it appears, was named after a go-getter, a railroad magnate and the first earth shaking reports we ever heard were from Jerry Baxter, blasting out the Tennessee Central right-of-way.

My Texas friend, Baxter, when we grew up, was a very likeable fellow and a great talker, but he was also the envy of the rest of us boys because he seemingly was born with a silver spoon in his mouth, while the rest of us had only a chop stick in ours. He owned a fine horse and buggy to travel around in, while we had to walk or ride a mule everywhere we went. I recall one dark night some of these boys came galloping up the highway toward a watermelon patch, when one of them on a mule ran into a pile of creek gravel that hadn't been spread. It caused the rider to go off over the critter's head and he started shouting to the other riders, "Catch him boys, Papa don't know I slipped him out of the stable." This started a Paul Revere ride back through Shackle Island to overtake and catch the mule so he could be returned to his stable.

Yesterday I received a letter from friend Baxter that gave me an awful shock. He had mailed it in one of his wife's personal envelopes with her name and address printed on it causing me to fear the worst had happened to him and that she was writing to tell about it. It was a great relief to find he had written it himself. In his letter he expressed great interest in the pictures of Shackle Island houses which appeared in the BANNER a short time ago. Here are some historical facts about this town.

For more than a hundred years it has been a farming and manufacturing center and was once owned entirely by Montgomery until a Hutchison married into the family and got possession of half of it. This newcomer cultivated the rich two hundred acre island in corn but didn't sell the corn nor feed it to stock, but made it into whiskey at a government sponsored still, then sold the whiskey. There is no record of any drunken brawls as a result of this still house. The nearest thing to it is the tale that one of the older Montgomerys would get so happy drinking the liquid fire that he would shout his approval of the whole Hutchison family by yelling, "Whoopee!" The sister married a man by that name and Jimmy Dick owned the still house.

Then all our lives we remember the old flour mill that sold Belle of Sumner flour and meal to several surrounding counties. So Shackle Island has always been a good place to live.

Here is a summary of the shape this country is in today. The highjackers have made it unsafe to ride airplanes, the railroaders are on strike, and the automobile will soon be ruled off the roads because they cause air pollution, which makes it imperative that we go back to horses and buggies. Baxter, since you are a direct descendant of the Montgomerys, we suggest that you come back to Shackle Island with one of your barrels of money and buy the whole town, then build a buggy factory. However, since we no longer have any buggy horses, you will also have to build a magnetic horse to pull these buggies. The buggies will have to be constructed with a metal dashboard in front so they will be attracted to the magnet in the horse and follow close behind. You can make these dashboards out of amalgamated beer cans. The horse could be made out of pulverized glass bottles firmly glued together and all these can be picked up beside every road in the country. There will also be a rolling manger at the end of the buggy shafts to hold a block of hay in front of the horse. Everything now is ready for you to start production, Baxter, except one thing, and we leave that problem for you to figure out. The Great problem is finding a way to put horse sense into the head of that magnetic horse so he will follow the hay scented manger anywhere you want to go.

The great advantage of this kind of conveyance is the magnet in the horse will jerk guns out of the hands and pockets of highjackers and trample them under the horses feet. It will also put Shackle Island back on the map for cleaning up the environment and you can spruce up the old ball diamond there and let them hold the World Series there.

Please give me credit, my dear friend in Texas, for writing you a long letter.

April 1, 1971
Goodlettsville Gazette

**Billy the Goat's
Tales of Two Towns
By L. D. R.**

Recently a young fellow was nice enough to stop and let me ride a short distance to the lower end of the farm. He was a newcomer around Shackle Island, and he asked me to write about the past history of his newly adopted metropolis.

Shackle Island is one of the two towns that caption this column, and a lot has been written the past few years about how its name Shackle *(printer appears to have left out a line at this point in the column)* nor has there ever been a prison in this locality, where prisoners were shackled. But the island is still there and comprises nearly 200 acres. Drakes Creek in the old days forked near the great Rock Castle up the creek, then flowed back together near St. John's Church, a mile or more below. The Long Hollow Pike runs across the middle of this island, with a bridge on each side.

Now as to how this village got its name we go back before the Revolutionary War. History says that our great, great grandfather, John McMurtry landed in Nashville on the boat with James Robertson and moved on out and settled at Shackle Island. He was living there before the war broke out, and he walked back and fought in it. He is buried in Beech Cemetery.

John McMurtry and his wife, Barbara, raised a family of boys in the latter part of the 1700's. If there were any girls I never heard of them. Anyway, a visitor came to his home one day looking for one of his sons, and his mother answered, "He has gone to shack on the island courting one of the girls."

This story has been handed down to me in the fifth generation by word of mouth. Another legend goes that later when the shack had seen its best days, someone remarked, "The old shack is getting awfully shackly, so we will call this place Shackle Island." If anyone can come up with a better answer as to why this place was so named, we'll be glad to hear it.

Shackle Island in the past has had some industry. Right after the Civil War there was a government still house there which made legal whiskey. It was owned by Jimmy Dick Hutchison and run by Burton Puryear. Then long before the Panama Canal was built there was a canal built at Shackle Island that ran along the New Hope Road for a mile.

It was called a mill race in my early days. It brought water from up the creek to turn a big wheel that powered a water mill where corn was ground into meal for farmers who brought in their turns of shelled corn on horseback. The old building still stands, but is now used for a barn. About 75 years ago the greatest industry of all came to Shackle Island when the Dorris Milling Company built the big flour mill. It transformed this town into one of the busiest in the whole county. That was back in mule team days, and wheat was hauled from several counties there to sell. It was made into Belle of Sumner flour and delivered to all stores as far away as Nashville by three big mules abreast to a big wagon. This big mill was powered by steam, and four foot cordwood was fed into the furnace to raise the steam. On Armistice Day in 1918 the fireman, W. A. Dorris, fed cordwood into it all day long and kept the steamboat whistle, that could be heard in several counties, blowing at five-minute intervals so everyone could know the war was over. We had no telephones or radios back then. The old mill is in shambles now.

There is one thing in Shackle Island that hasn't changed one bit in the last 100 years, and that is the Robert Worsham General Store. It's still going strong, with the third Robert running it now, and the fourth Robert just out of the Army and ready to take over at any time.

This town used to have a splendid baseball diamond with many good ball players, and to us Sumner Countians, at least, the "world series" was held there every summer.

Here is hoping that the young fellow who lives in the ancient rock castle who wanted something written about Shackle Island will get enlightenment and pleasure out of my feeble efforts to oblige him. However, I wonder if he really realizes how near he lives to the jumping off place, which is a sheer cliff along the creek above his house. Mr. Montgomery, the former owner, once had a watermelon patch on the hill above the cliff and one day two fellows invaded the patch. When they saw the owner approaching they ran to this high cliff and slid down it, each with a melon under his arm. They escaped with only a few stone bruises up and down their backs.

July 8, 1971
Goodlettsville Gazette

Billy the Goat's Tales of Two Towns By L. D. R.

This time I fear this corny column may have a sour note in it for you who read it, which is the reason it was not turned in to be printed last week. It is the story of how one of my first writings for paper nearly three score years ago backfired on me.

I started writing for and got my "diploma in journalism" over the telephone from a very distinguished editor who later became U. S. Ambassador to Finland and whose very name signified intelligence. The year I became 21 a friend and I went to Pueblo, Colorado where we had a job waiting for us with the largest concern in the West. The company owned a big department store, a whole mining town, and the railroad that ran up the mountains into the town where six months before Stone City was founded. Residents lived in tents and when business opened up they produced fine building stone.

When I had worked there about a week the president of the giant concern sent me out to Stone City to help the manager run the store. This was a lucky break for me because I got to see the West in the raw. Not knowing a soul there I started writing letters to the *Gallatin News* describing what life was like for a tenderfoot like me in this frontier mining town. The editor printed these letters and when I returned home the next year, I continued to write whenever something of interest occurred. A neighbor told about killing a monstrous big snake that his small dog treed and I wrote about it. It was printed also and made an astounding story that other county papers copied. That winter, after an all day hunt, a big gray wolf was slain after he had killed a grown sheep the previous night. This was with thanks to Old Casey, the Collie dog, that followed the wolf all day barking at him, when all the other dogs tucked their tails and ran when the wolf made at them snarling.

The hunters could never get close enough to shoot the wolf but late that afternoon Casey treed him in a hollow log, where the hunters killed him. The tired hunters allowed me to take their catch to Shackle Island to show him. While there I phoned this distinguished editor of the *News* and told him about the wolf and he asked, "What did you say your name is?" Again, I told him my name and he answered, "You will have to get someone to vouch for the truth of what you are telling." I called Mr. Lon Hunter to the phone and he declared I was telling the truth for the wolf was there at his feet. He added, "Anything this boy tells you to your face you can believe, just beware of what he writes."

This taught me a lesson which was never tell a tall tale on anyone and identify him by name like I did in this case, for this man spent two weeks on jury service and they quizzed him about the story. He told them that the snake didn't actually swallow the little dog but was big enough to and probably would if he hadn't killed it.

During all this time the editor and I had never met, however, a year or two later we did meet on very high ground. I was up in my peach orchard on the top most part of Vertical Plains when up around that winding half-mile road walked the Honorable Edward Albright of the *Gallatin News*, electioneering for State Senator.

I told him he had certainly earned my vote by climbing up that hill seeking it. Then I added, "Of course, you will not believe me when I declare I'm going to vote for you." "Why not," he quickly asked. I answered, "Because I'm the rascal you wouldn't believe about the wolf."

I've often wondered if he climbed that high hill not knowing who he was going to meet or did he know when he started up and just wanted to know what a notorious liar looked like. Anyway, I voted for him for I held no malice toward him for he taught me a great lesson about writing an exaggerated story.

Hind sight is no good of course, but in telling that tall tale instead of using my real neighbor's name, had I said my neighbor, Bill Breezeley, he never would have gotten put on that jury to give me a hard time.

September 23, 1971
Goodlettsville Gazette

Billy the Goat's
Tales of Two Towns
By L. D. R.

It seems that sometimes you wonder how a feeble mind exerts energy and fodder enough to write this stuff, so for that reason the column will switch to memory lane and start a series about an 80-year-old rat race for survival in a land of plenty. The beginning of this race is left completely blank, because I don't remember being born in a log cabin and living there the first few years of my existence. This house was located in Long Hollow, in the forks where Bland Pass and Lick Hollow rivulets run together, but a few years ago it was moved down the pike a mile and now stands on the farm of Aubrey Moore.

However, I do remember as well as if it was yesterday, riding on the wagon loaded with household furniture with my younger brother and Uncle Tom, as our parents moved to the newly built house a mile up the highway. I must have been around three years old at the time, and evidently didn't like the looks of that new house. I ran away from home that very day without ever coming back there to live for more than a dozen years, which may sound ridiculous but nevertheless is true.

Grandpa and Grandma lived right across the road, and there I took up my abode. This old Rebel had a corn field and peach orchard on top of one of the highest hills where I first learned high farming.

Down a ways on the east hillside, a great pleasure always awaited me at this season of the year that youths today will never be permitted to enjoy. I picked up chestnuts under the giant chestnut trees that were there. A number of years ago the blight destroyed all of these trees.

Later on, before we were even teenagers, my brother and I started out in a small way to make a million dollars. We scoured the woods hunting and cutting hoop poles and dragging them out to where we could get to them with a wagon. Then we hauled them to the cooper shop, the only factory in Goodlettsville and sold them for about a cent-and-a-half apiece. We never made a million, but a wagon load of them would bring about a thousand pennies of course, and we thought we were getting rich!

These hickory hoop poles were made into hoops to go around flour barrels, for back then everybody kept a barrel of flour in the kitchen. For bread they ate homemade biscuits and used a lot of flour in making gravy.

Today we read about much unemployment, which is a reminder that laziness is the mother of invention. Every time a new machine is invented, it knocks thousands of people out of work in this country. Many pleasant memories I have about going with the thresher each summer that employed a lot of men to cut and shock the grain then thresh it. Now in the modern age, one man on a reaper can do all this work by himself, while another fellow in a truck comes along and picks up the sacks of grain. Furthermore, back in the good old days it took a lot of hands to cut and shock a big field of hay, then haul it on a wagon to the barn, or more often stack it out in the field to wait for the mule-powered baler to get there and bale it. Each Fall when I was young and stout, my job was tying wires on those ninety-pound bales and packing them away and stacking two hundred or more each day. It took several of us and two big mules to run that baler, but it was fun and gave us an appetite and made us sleep at night. Today one man rides a baler and does all this, but leaves the bales scattered all over the field, not stacked up like we left them. Then a tarpaulin has to be put out over them if it starts raining. So which is progress?

September 30, 1971
Goodlettsville Gazette

Billy the Goat's Tales of Two Towns By L. D. R.

Continuing from last week, this column is about the rat race and my running away from home when three years old. It seems it is time for a gadabout to return home, so here is how it happened: By the time I was old enough to go to school I already knew how to use a hammer and saw, and earned spending money building chicken coops and feed pens for my grandmothers and aunt. When I reached my middle teens I was a full fledged carpenter, but nobody believed it. For instance, the village blacksmith hired me to help him build a barn. We set one row of posts, and I told him we would have to square the bar up with my stool square and line before we could set the other rows. But he and his farm hand, an elderly man, gave me the horse laugh, and said he didn't care whether it was square or not.

I was too much of a kid to argue with two men older than my daddy, so I let them find out I was right the hard way. When we put the tin roof on, it saw-toothed two inches at the eves and comb. The blacksmith blinked his eyes and said, "Boy, I thought you were a carpenter."

About this same time my younger brother and I remodeled our parent's home, and made it more than twice as big as when first built. When we began the job our father hired a traveling clock fixer to help us start off right, but he didn't know B from beef foot about carpentering. In fact, he knew little about clocks also. One day he was working on old Uncle Phil's clock, and it started striking. This clock mechanic couldn't get it stopped, and he panicked and left in a hurry, telling the old

fellow that maybe it would stop when it ran down.

Anyway, we two boys finished the house to show them we could, and I moved back home with an upstairs room all to myself, and a parlor below for my sisters. The house still stands today with its dormer windows like the old style houses. It's new owners have brick veneered it, making it the most beautiful place in all of Long Hollow.

After this job, I, with a man much older, started making cross ties back in the woods, which was the hardest work I ever did in my whole life, and it was the turning point of my career. But that is a long story and will have to wait for another time.

Among the jobs I have held and haven't retired from yet is one I acquired only recently when I started running a one-patient nursing home here at Vertical Plains. My patient is the same one who came into my life as a pretty little hitchhiker who I picked up on her way to church with a group of other youngsters. That was years ago, and I had never met or heard of her until that day. We were properly introduced by the two elderly spinsters whose house I was remodeling. It all started when I arrived for work one morning and inquired who the plump little miss was who I spied in the woman's corner at church the night before. These spinsters told me who she was, then began praising her so much that I thought she must be a princess from back in the hills, but didn't expect to ever see her again. However, late in the afternoon while I was still at work, here came both of my employers out of the door yelling, "Here comes Hester!" And as I looked up, a group of youngsters were coming by on their way to church.

As the group came up they promptly called to Hester to come in a moment and then called me, where they introduced us. I was startled out of my wits, but managed to tell Hester that if she would wait until I changed my clothes she could ride to church with me. She accepted, and told the others to go on. Now, after 55 years she keeps me waiting on her 24 hours per day, because she can't walk, and has to be carried around in a wheel chair.

However, I persevere in attending to her, because I don't want her or any of our offspring to ever think she drove her ducks to a bad market, when she stepped in that buggy with me that night in the long ago.

Tomorrow she plans to go to Manchester for our grandson Martin Harmon's wedding, and I'll go along with the wheel chair.

October 14, 1971
Goodlettsville Gazette

**Billy the Goat's
Tales of Two Towns
By L. D. R.**

Reminiscing about my old stomping grounds past and present, Long Hollow, today, looks exactly like it did 75 years ago when I first remembered it. But in my life time these steep hills have been cleared and cultivated in tobacco and sometimes in watermelons, while the flat tops of the hills were planted in large peach orchards, which produced bountiful crops of fine peaches, back in the days when they didn't need spraying every week to control brown rot and other diseases. Then the tractor replaced the horse and the bull tongue plow and were worthless on the hillsides and stumpy new grounds. So today these rich, fertile hill fields are covered with a dense young forest, and now they look exactly like they did in my younger days.

At the beginning of this period Uncle Dan Elam lived in Long Hollow on a fairly level farm with a high steep hill directly across the highway in front of his house. He had some grown daughters. One day a romantic young fellow said to him, "Uncle Dan, if you will give me Miss Sue I will dig that big hill for you." The deal didn't go through, but if it had, that lover with a pick and shovel would have had to live longer than Methuselah. Today, A. A. McDuffee owns that hill and has started digging it down with a bulldozer. But he doesn't plan to dig it all down, for he would have no place to put it. He plans to build a house to live in at the foot of the north hillside, which is a unique place to live. There is a cave spring just back of the house, which will furnish plenty of water, and the family can get snow cream almost half of the year,

for the sun will have a major job melting any snow that falls there. Why can't we all have a nice cool spring for drinking water and quit washing our faces with and drinking river water?

These enchanting hills used to be exciting to prowl over when we would hear the cluck of buggies and wagons in the valley below us and hear roosters crowing and ducks and geese quacking at most every farm house we looked down on. It was especially an exciting day when Goodlettsville's popular merchant Cricket Galbreath, out squirrel hunting, reported seeing a big wolf in these hills. Nobody believed it, except two elderly men who went possum hunting one night, the same night that two mischievous boys were also out hunting. These boys were on a high ridge when we heard the men talking loudly in a deep hollow below us and we recognized who they were. Then we blew out our lantern to keep them from knowing anyone else was in the woods, and we began running around the hillside through the dry leaves and brush, screaming at the top of our voice like a wild cat.

One of them said, "Listen—that's that d-n wolf." Four booms of their double barrel muzzle loading shot guns rang out. We heard the spent shot peppering down on the leaves below us. Their four dogs left them and headed for home, barking in fright. We knew it would take five minutes for them to reload, and one of us ran down the hill towards them, screaming. At that these two brave hunters took off after their dogs, shouting "Here, here," and they fired caps on their guns to scare the wolf away as they ran.

The view from the tops of these hills can fool a person. The story goes that Uncle Billy Buck, who lived on a level farm at the head of Long Hollow, but had a hill pasture across the road, went after his cows one evening and his daughter went with him. They went around the hill and climbed from the far side. When they reached the high knob their house was in plain sight of them, the daughter asked, "Who lives down ther?" Uncle Billy answered, "Aunt Polly Squibba, she's a nice lady. We'll go down to see her if you want to." So they did, and the daughter didn't know she was back home until she entered the house and saw her mother.

In all these years only one mishap ever occurred in these hills. That happened to Beemer, the Dutchman, who was hired to come to America and fight with the Yankees. He was knocked unconscious while out getting wood. But it's best to let him tell it his way: "I fell and rolled the hill down and didn't know myself anymore."

March 2, 1972
Goodlettsville Gazette

Billy the Goat's
Tales of Two Towns
By L. D. R.

Last week I received a letter from my granddaughter in Santa Cruz, California enclosing subscription money for me to have this paper sent to her and her husband, being recently married.

She stated that they want to read this column. How can anything be written in it that would interest that young fellow who lives and grew up in that modernistic part of the world and who perhaps never dreamed of the corny things that happen back in the sticks, where I've lived all my life? I will make a try of it by writing these two a long letter.

My dear Janet and Husband, now that for the last two weeks you have been briefed on China and the customs of these ancient people, maybe you would like to be briefed on Vertical Plains where the sun only shines every other day in clear weather and the children all grew up unrestrained like blackberries out in the pastures.

Yes, the only thing they were taught here at home was that "a good run was better than a bad stand" and they were very apt pupils and soon learned that themselves, for every time one of them got a little rowdy and I reached for a switch they would outrun me until I stopped and started laughing, which proves a good scare was better than a beating.

Maybe I did lambast one or two of them, for which I have always been sorry that they didn't outrun me. However, that way of training children sometimes backfired, like the time I was milking a cow that was hard to milk. I fed her in a stall that had a hole on one side of it and I gave the oldest boy a stick and told him that if the cow started out to knock her horns off. Well, just as I got the bucket full she kicked it out of my hands and lunged toward the hole and the boy dropped the stick and beat it for the house, the cow right behind him. I picked up the stick and started out behind them, but his mother out at the wood pile saw me and yelled, "Let the boy alone or I'll brain you with a stick of stove wood," causing a laughing retreat by me.

When the second boy, whom you know well, started to school, although only six years old, I knew he was too mature minded to put up with the kid stuff and preferred to fraternize with grown people, so I told him if things got to where he couldn't handle them to come straight home. The very next day a grown friend of his came walking by the school playground and hollered out his name, he ran out to the road and talked with him a few minutes. When he returned to the playground one little boy yelled, "Look at old Jimbo trying to act big, let's put him in the toilet hole," and quickly four of them grabbed him by the arms and were carrying him toward the outdoor toilet. When some of the older boys, including his brother, made the little boys release him, he headed straight for home. When the older children came home from school that day, they said the schoolmarm declared she was going to whip their little brother for leaving school without permission.

"No," I told her the next morning, "he did exactly what I told him to do and besides he knew that his mamma could keep a gang of rowdies from humiliating him like they did even if his teacher couldn't."

Later my Sunday School teacher, who happened to be State Superintendent of Education, told me she had no cause to whip him and that the other boys were the ones she should have whipped. But I told her not to whip them either because they were only joking and he just didn't like that kind of joke.

This about tells the humorous side of raising children here at Vertical Plains, except one day I heard the youngest one of them all shout to his two little sisters, "I'll kill you" and I plunked him on top of the head with my thumb which made him so mad he whirled on me like we was going to annihilate me. That was another time I had to do the running.

Janet, I don't know how long I will be able to write this column. My eyes are getting dim, but thank goodness I am not nearsighted like the Gardner family who lived near us in bygone days. Mr. Gardner, a prominent farmer, who was nearsighted had two sons named, Sam and Silas, and when church services were held on Sunday nights these boys and their father were usually there.

At the dim lighted church in those days the men stood outside and talked before the services began. One of these boys would approach his father and say, "Hello, Mr. Gardner, where are Sam and Silas tonight?" "Around here somewhere," the old gentleman would answer. Then his son would ask for a chew of tobacco and on being handed a twist of tobacco by his father he would break the twist half into and say, "Thank you, Mr. Gardner," as he handed back half of the tobacco.

Mr. Gardner had a sister who lived with him. She was also nearsighted and was fast becoming an old maid, a fact she laid to her poor eyesight because she had had several beaux but none of them ever popped the question. Finally, another fellow made a date to come to see her one Sunday afternoon and she wanted to convince him her eyes were alright so she took a needle and stuck it in the front gate post some distance from the house. When her new beau arrived she entertained him out on the shady front porch while their big old yellow cat purred around their feet. As the evening wore on and she thought they would soon be called to supper, She said, "I believe I see a needle sticking in that gatepost." Sure enough, when her new suitor ran to the gate he found the needle and was impressed. They were called in to supper to eat the delicious food she had prepared for him. She spied the big yellow pitcher full of buttermilk in the middle of the table and yelled, "Scat you old rascal!" as she slapped the pitcher off the table onto the floor.

August 24, 1972
Goodlettsville Gazette

Billy the Goat's Tales of Two Towns By L. D. R.

If you have been missing this column for the last few weeks, it's dog days, and all Nature seems to be asleep. Who can have enthusiasm enough to think of anything to write about except gobs of gloom? Besides, nobody has energy enough to do anything humorous or sensational that is worth writing about.

Here in the country, a lone Bob White whistles occasionally to break the monotony. The mocking bird has stopped singing around the nest in the thorn tree, and the jay birds no longer call out "half" in the orchard, because they have picked all the fruit or caused it to fall off.

Dog days are a spooky time for the Republicans to hold a convention. Their elephant may go to sleep this drowsy weather, but I hope the Democratic donkey will stay awake and keep braying. There seems to be several Republicans in Tennessee today, so no offense is meant toward them. I am a dyed in the wool Democrat. When I grew up there was only one Republican near Shackle Island, a red whiskered fellow, who was the victim of all the boys' pranks. One night they drove all his cows in the barn and took the bells off them. With these bells they invaded the corn field in the creek bottom near his house. Out he came to chase the cows from the cornfield. When he got near one of the boys the boy would quit ringing the bell, and another boy would start ringing in another part of the field. That way they kept the old fellow chasing cows until daylight.

The only time I ever admired anything about this breed of politicians was when I met one of their daughters, but that young lady has been one of the strongest Democrats in the world for more than half a century, and I still admire her.

Without changing the subject, a Republican is responsible for the heading of this column. He delighted in getting me before a crowd and telling them how ignorant I was, then telling them that if he thought he had one drop of Ralph blood in him he would take his knife and cut it out, which amused me as much as any of the other fellows, because he was opening the gate for me to turn the tables on him.

Luckily, he was in my carpenter shop when the editor of the GOODLETTSVILLE GAZETTE came in and asked me to write a column for the first edition of the paper. I told him I would, and after he left, my Republican good friend asked, "What are you going to write about?" I answered, "I'm going to write about you." Well, sire, he fell into a furious rage and yelled, "I just double dare you to put my name in that paper." This was incentive enough for me to write a good story that made him wish I had told his name when I told how smart he was. I wrote that my fellow worker was the smartest millwright in Tennessee, and I had to call him for anything that got wrong with one of my woodworking machines. Then he had to go to the office and tell our boss that he had been fixing that Billy Goat's machine, as he always called me. Then he would tell the boss he was worth a million dollars to the company, and that when he passed away he wanted them to take his brain and put it in alcohol and set it on the counter in the office for people to look at. I described him so well everybody knew who I was talking about by letting him brag on himself. Then I signed the column, "The Billy Goat." The paper put the picture of a goat at the top causing a lot of readers to refer to me as "The Old Goat" when I neither have whiskers nor long hair, nor do I eat briars for a living, even though I do pick the berries from the vine and enjoy them.

Thanks to vacation time between schools, this week has been enjoyable one for us two inmates here at Vertical Plains. Our children from two western capitals are here visiting us. The first to arrive was the Hawkins family, Juanita and her husband and daughter Annelle from Oklahoma City, and then our son James T. and wife and their two daughters from Sacramento, California. They were all here with some of the local children to sing "Happy Birthday" to their mama. But they will soon be leaving to get back to school, where some of them are on the college faculties and the two younger girls are in school.

Although we enjoyed their visit very much, the thing that hurts is seeing them leave to go back home, because it may be a long time before they visit us on another vacation.

Did you know there are some folks who can't take a joke? This brings to mind a Mr. Pigue, a veteran joker, who bought a farm at Shackle Island and moved to it from Nashville back in the horse and buggy days. He left several well-to-do friends in town who acquired automobiles as they came on the market. They drove out often to see this old friend on the farm. A wealthy merchant friend and his wife came several times, and one day their joker host told them that out in a thicket pasture was an old graveyard. A ground hog had dug a hole down into one of the graves for his den. The farmer told them that if they would hold their ear down close to this hole they would hear a voice saying, "Nothing, nothing."

To hear this uncanny phenomenon the city folks made a trek to the graveyard, and came back telling their host that they listened intently with their ear down to the hole and heard nothing.

Then the joker laughed and said, "I told you a voice would say nothing."

The upset of it all was these two city folks became furious, they bawled out their host for pulling such a joke on them and they never came back for another visit.

November 23, 1972
Goodlettsville Gazette

Billy the Goat's
Tales of Two Towns
By L. D. R.

The election is over and we two here at Vertical Plains lost our vote, because so many voters were so sympathetic and obliging and liked firecrackers so well, they thought the people of Southeast Asia would enjoy fireworks displays another four years. Another reason is that the Republican political machine is such a well greased piece of machinery, a fact this younger generation is not acquainted with like we oldtimers. Back in bygone days everybody used axle grease to grease their buggies and wagons to make them run smooth. Also, if their children developed a deep cold they relieved it by greasing their chests with polecat grease. Now the question is which of these two lubricants did this winning party use in their campaign. As you know, the eavesdropping affair and the instant peace rumors have a very offensive odor to them. You be the judge. Another striking thing about all this is where they got all this grease, as one of the main cogs in their efficient machine is a product of a dictator country named Greece. So, was it imported or did it originate in the land of the free and home of the brave?

However, the most contradicting thing about the campaign is one of the leading candidates in the race consistently avowed he was against busing, but the morning after the election, the paper showed this same fellow apparently in the act of bussing his better-half in their victory celebration. We know that no one in the human family is against bussing if confronted by the right lips in a time of rejoicing.

Anyway, we can all be assured that this country is not going to the dogs during the next four years because most everybody has gone to the ball games either in their living rooms or the ball parks.

If the World Series had been going on all day the seventh of November, it is doubtful if either of the candidates would have polled enough votes to elect him constable.

Back several decades ago, when I was growing up we all went to the dogs or else had them come to us, because at that time nobody had a radio or television to entertain them nor even an automobile to visit distant friends or relatives. In every neighborhood in the country farmers had packs of hounds, and if it wasn't raining or too cold these farmers would get together two or three times a week to have a fox race. All the shut-ins who didn't feel like going along had to do was step out on the porch, listen to the music, as the dogs chased the fox over the hills and across the fields near their homes.

During my whole life the only man whom I ever hoodwinked anything of value out of without paying him for it was a veteran fox hunter, who it is told would blow his fox horn at dusk and take his pack of hounds to the woods and jump a fox. Then he would stay out all night listening to the race and, if the race was still on at daylight he would run back home and drink a cup of coffee and grab some meat and bread then run back to the dogs.

No, my conscience doesn't hurt me one bit for the way I did him, for after all he came out better in the long run as it gave him more time to chase foxes because it left him with one less daughter to feed.

Now a word about this fox hunter's daughter, who in the minds of her dozen and half grandchildren is a millionaire, because she keeps tab on all their birthdays and sends all of them a dollar bill on each occasion. Now she is deeper and deeper in her philanthropy because next year come the birthday of her great grandson and she will have to send him a two dollar bill leaving me a Scrooge in all their minds.

When I grew up no one ever gave me a penny on my birthday except once back in the foremost part of my memory. Boolin Hoolin taught me, a baby on his knee, to call him that which were the first words I ever remember speaking. Later on I learned he gave me two twenty dollar gold pieces which my mother kept until I was old enough to go to business college and there I paid my tuition. But a few decades later he got his money's worth by using me as a human guinea pig to test a quart of wildcat whiskey to see if it would kill me before he drank any of it. I had laryngitis from setting out shade trees in February and stopped by his house and asked him in a whisper, the only way I could talk, for a drink of the wildcat whiskey. He exclaimed, "I grannies, it will kill you," because he had given the fellow he had sent after it a drink of it which made him deathly sick. But I knew and he didn't know that the fellow had drunk a whole quart of the stuff he had bought for himself before he took this drink and that's what hurt him.

I told the old timer that I had no business living when I couldn't talk, so he poured me out a half a glass of the moonshine and when I drank it, it flew to my head and I told him I had to hurry on home to do some work.

He said he would ride down home with me but he never knew why the old T Model was seesawing from one side of the road to the other. He probably thought I was dodging mud holes, when I was drunk as a biled owl, the only time I was ever drunk in my whole life.

Arriving home, I told him to go on in the house and picked up my grubbing hoe and went out and dug up a plant bed. When I finished the job I was perfectly sober and could call in the hogs a mile away, for that wildcat liquor or the work with the grubbing hoe had cured my laryngitis completely.

I figure that this old timer, being able to drink the moonshine for medical purposes without any fear of getting poisoned was worth the $40 he gave me when a baby, especially when I had to get drunk to prove it.

November 30, 1972
Goodlettsville Gazette

Billy the Goat's
Tales of Two Towns
By L. D. R.

Until recently I thought I had seen everything there is to see in Goodlettsville, where I ran a carpenter's shop half of my life. Then daughter Evelyn visited us one evening and carried us down the Two Mile Pike to see that conglomeration of stores across from where the old railroad track ran to Edgefield Junction. We went in the uppermost entrance and found a broad street under roof, with stores on each side of it, then started down the street where the most we saw on display were women's wearing apparel in all the bright colors of Joseph's coat, and I concluded that if they sell all these garments in the next twenty-five years, the population explosion will have to be quadrupled and a million baby girls raised up to buy them.

By the time we reached the other end of this street I hadn't found any old fashioned long handled men's underpants, but was told to go to Roebuck's three miles away to get them. I already felt like I had walked five miles, but we started back toward where we entered and I saw a sign that said, "save 99 cents here," making me feel pretty good for I had saved a whole dollar by not spending a penny.

Why that place is even bigger than B. F. Myers dry-goods store and Crickett Galbreath's grocery store combined fifty years ago, and not as easy to find things you want to buy, for Crickett was the most accommodating merchant this town ever had.

In the summer season he kept a wagon load of roasting ears piled up in the middle of the floor. When asked how he sold it he would answer, "Ten cents a dozen if I sack it or twenty cents if you sack it yourself," which was a business way to sell it for he knew the customer would shuck down half the pile trying to find the best ears.

Now of all things, I've just come from the mail box with a fifty page catalogue from one of these new stores we visited that evening, and in it are several pages advertising diamonds of all kinds and several more pages displaying rings and still more pages showing watches. Had I known about this place I could have spent my whole dollar buying a black diamond file that we need here on the farm to sharpen hoes and axes, and also a box of hog rings to put in hogs' noses to keep them from rooting up the fence and getting out. As for needing a watch, I already have a half dozen or more. I call them all Crystal because they are always on the watch to keep me from packing leaves in on my feet or throwing down on the floor that twisted Gordian knot on light bread that cause me to nearly starve before I can get them off.

These gloomy rainy Sundays there is nothing for us two shut-ins to do except listen to a sermon on TV and the most interesting one is preached by Dr. Simmons, who says that all denominations must pull together if this old world is ever to get spinning in the right direction. However, the only preacher I ever heard that backed up what he preached was in the wild and wooly west. That was the year I was twenty—one and clerking in a store in Stone City back in the Rocky Mountains. Late one Saturday afternoon I rode the train to Pueblo to visit my friend who came west with me and who clerked in the main store there. He was still at work when I arrived, so, waiting for closing time, I happened to step out on a side street by the store. Out there a Salvation Army Captain was preaching to a large crowd of men, where some of them were smoking cigarettes near him. Twice he asked them to quit blowing smoke in his face, but they never stopped. Finally the Captain yelled out, "I can whip any cigarette smoker in Pueblo," and a big fellow on the outskirts of the crowd yelled back, "Old man, you are taking in too d—n much territory."

Instantly, the Captain threw off his coat and answered, "Come ahead if you want to fight," and when the fellow nudged his way through the crowd and got there one of the fiercest fist fights I ever saw began.

Before the battle was over a policeman appeared and arrested the fellow and put him in the patrol wagon, then told the Captain to get in too as a witness against the disturber. Then the wagon pulled away with the Captain singing, "Happy on the Way."

When the subject is preachers though at this season of the year the most unforgettable one moved into the house at Old Beech in 1905, and for several Thanksgivings he sponsored a rabbit hunt with the boys and sticks and dogs, the only way to have fun rabbit hunting and the safest way for no one to get shot for no guns were allowed.

When a rabbit jumped up in the open field and forty dogs and forty boys took after it from all sides. That preacher could out run any of them until the rabbit was captured and put in a sack for the few men on horseback, who came to see the fun, to carry.

We usually got 30 to 40 rabbits each hunt and the rabbits were barbecued on an open pit by an expert. Then we all turned out that night hungry to eat them.

This preacher knew how to handle all animals on the farm from the smallest to the most ferocious. This fact he owes his life to or he wouldn't have been there to go hunting with us boys.

He grew up on a farm near Murfreesboro and he, being the oldest son, had to look after the farm while his father served as Governor of Tennessee. One day an old sow farrowed a litter of pigs back under the big corn crib beside the barn. One day the future preacher crawled up under the crib to count the pigs while his younger brother waited outside. When he neared the bed of pigs the old sow lunged at him with her mouth open to chew his face to pieces and nothing could he get hold of to fight her off. Having a chew of tobacco in his mouth, he let go a mouth full of amber into her eyes and the angry old animal ran out squealing like she had been shot.

Billy the Goat's
Tales of Two Towns
By L. D. R.

Being in no mood this time to write a humorous column, there is only one subject on my mind, which you will soon discover what it is and why. I will begin by asking a question. Back before writing paper and slates were invented what did people do their arithmetic on? The answer is they multiplied on the face of the earth and so did chickens, for that matter, so my subject is chickens and children.

When my lifetime partner and I started our connubial venture, we devoted our time for over two years to raising chickens, then our first baby arrived, which changed our attitudes toward life completely. Now that the first baby is in Vanderbilt Hospital where she has undergone surgery for arthritis, I am depressed.

Here are some fond memories of these children that linger on my mind. They were all born about a year and half after each other, first two girls and a boy, then two more girls and a boy. We thought that was all, but half a dozen years later we got badly or goodly fooled. Two more girls and a boy came seeking admission with the rest of them.

Of course today, with all this family planning and pills, a big family like that is taboo, but back then the more the merrier.

Away back when I was a half grown boy Haley's Comet with its fiery tail was visible in the sky causing people to fear it would destroy this Earth. I dreamed that the world was coming to end a certain day in May and never slept any that night I was so scared. Years

later our first baby was born on that very date in May.

Raising a bevy of children proved to be a great incentive for working hard to provide for them and also a barrel of fun. However, the fun backfired on me one time and ended in a sudden shock.

The four oldest children used to follow me around everywhere I went and one evening at dusk or nearly dark, we were all walking by a vacant house beside the pike, when I thought I would have some fun out of them. I told them that was where the old catawampus lived and that I would throw a rock against the house to wake him up, little dreaming that when the rock hit the house, bedlam would break loose inside, but it did to my great surprise.

I scared a drove of hogs bedded down for the night, and out they ran, all of them squealing, "Boo Boo." I started running like I was scared as the two youngest children had already started ahead of me. When we got down about fifty yards, one of the older daughters, thinking all the rest of us were ahead of her, glanced back over her shoulder and saw another sister running toward her in the dark. She thought it was one of the boogers she had heard coming out of the old house. She began screaming in fright like I had never heard a child scream before or since. This brought me to a sudden stop, and I had an awful time convincing her that there was no such thing as a catawampus and that it was only a frightened bunch of hogs she heard. Anyway, that broke me from ever trying to scare them anymore.

The youngest three children, though, brought on the most fun I ever had in my whole life. The two youngest daughters are now married and are professional pianists, a talent they never inherited from their parents, for neither of us can play *Yankee Doddle* on a French harp. For their success playing the piano at weddings, cantatas, and horse shows they are indebted to their talented music teacher who moved into our midst when they were little girls.

Here is the story: They were having a Christmas program at Madison Creek School one night in which the six older children were participating. With their mother, I carried them all to the school that night and then drove on to Goodlettsville to buy some groceries. When I arrived back there and parked my car, the music teacher and her husband drove up and parked beside my car. I introduced myself to them and we all went in together. When we got inside the house was full and we three had to sit on the very back seat. Pretty soon the music teacher, sitting between me and her husband, exclaimed, "Look at that lady up near the stage with those three little children, one in her lap and two standing beside her." Then pretty soon one of the other children went to the lady in the chair to get clothes fixed then another and another. The music teacher made a remark each time about her having so many children.

Finally she asked me, "How many children does she have, do you know?" I answered, "I think she has nine." She exclaimed, "I bet her husband is not worth killing or he would be up there helping her tend to them." I told her she was exactly right about the fellow being not worth killing, while I tried to keep a straight face to keep from laughing. Then she turned to me and asked, "Who is she, do you know?" I answered Yes, mam, she is my wife." Punching me in the ribs with her elbow, she yelled, "You need killing!" and I answered, "No, mam, I don't. You've done bet your money that I wasn't worth killing and I don't want you to lose any money on me."

The new acquaintances became our best neighbors and I shall never forget how we met.

Billy the Goat's
Tales of Two Towns
By L. D. R.

Here are some corny happenings that Shackle Islanders laughed about in bygone days: The fabled Dick Hullett, about whom there has been so much told, was a share cropper on a 600 acre plantation that extended from Long Hollow Pike to beyond Happy Hollow. His wife smoked a pipe. For smoking tobacco she depended on their landlord who raised the weed for his own use. One day she sent her son Jimmy to him for another supply. Jimmy said to him, "Mr. Montgomery, Mammy said please sir send her a smoke." The old gentleman, tired of keeping her in tobacco all the time, exclaimed, "Well, don't your Mammy do anything but smoke?" To this the young fellow replied, "Yes sir—sometimes she chaws."

Then there was the well-known famer who with his wife one cold night walked out across the pasture to a party at a neighbor's where a bottle was passed around freely. When they got back home that night, chilled through and through, he began building a fire in the open fireplace. When his wife noticed how he was standing the wood up, with one end sticking up the chimney instead of laying it across the dog irons as he should have done, she yelled at him, "Put that wood on there right, sir. You know that's not the way to build a fire."

"Yes, it is. Burn it the way it grows," he answered.

The Long Hollow Pike is one subject that has never been written about, and few know about it today. Originally it followed the buffalo trail down Long Hollow, and for two miles it came down the branch, either in it, or on its banks, then made a right turn along the line where today the farms of Oscar Malone and Bennett Ralph join. It continued in a straight line over two low hills to Madison Creek, and across where today all that remains of that old road is a quarter of a mile of wide, hard surface road to Patton Branch. This, in bygone days, was the center of the old Sixth District of Sumner County, with a church and a school house, too, where I attended school for four sessions. Memories are all that are left of the days when Atch was sent to the spring after a bucket of water, and caught a big bull frog, which escaped off his desk and went hopping up towards the teacher, causing a lot of laughter and confusion. Thence the road continued on through a low gap where the rock quarry is today, and on across the arched bridge over Manskers Creek and on to Goodletts Store, near Pin Hood stagecoach.

Then four enterprising gentlemen, Messer Tom Clark, Frank Taylor, Jim Cantrell and Bob Cartwright, built the turnpike over steep Cantrell Hill and put a tollgate on it. I remember the four men well, but not when they built the road. The first toll gate was in Davidson County near the present I-65, but when tollgates were put out of that county, they moved the gate over the hill into Sumner County. The only gatekeeper they ever had in this county was Bill Aton, an old bachelor who lived at the tollgate house with his spinster sister, Annie, who helped collect the toll.

These two were always out on the porch to raise the gate and hold out their hand for the money when they heard a vehicle or horseback rider approaching, except on two occasions: One night a load of young people left Shackle Island on a hay ride on a two horse wagon by way of Hendersonville and up Two Mile Pike to Goodlettsville, then out Long Hollow. It was late in the night when Bill heard them coming. He thought it was a lumber wagon coming from Nashville, and out he came in his shirt tail, but when he heard all of the girls on the wagon giggling and screaming, he released the rope that let the gate up and beat it back into the house. So the driver drove on through and kept his quarter in his pocket.

Miss Annie, diminutive and wrinkled as she was, got in tough with a fellow up north through a marriage bureau. He was looking for a wife. They corresponded for awhile. Then Beau Brummel asked her to send him her picture. But she didn't. Instead, she sent him a picture of the girl who lived on the farm across the pike, who was plump and pretty as a peach. This evidently set the northern suitor wild, for he boarded a train, got off in Goodlettsville, went to Newbern's Livery Stable and hired a horse and buggy, then drove out to the tollgate.

It so happened that Miss Annie came out to collect the toll that day. The fellow stopped and said, "I want to see Miss Annie."

"I'm Miss Annie," she answered.

"Getup, there!" the fellow exclaimed as he slapped his horse and turned around to drive back to Goodlettsville.

When I was about half grown I got my first job on public works. It was operating a rock crusher, making little rocks out of big ones, for the Long Hollow Turnpike Co. This machine was the latest model of its day, and was a round hammer, the size and shape of a fat doughnut, only a lot heavier, with which I sat on a stool and beat these rocks for so much a square yard for beating them and piling them up in a pile a foot high.

Back then there were no laws against child labor and no freeze on how much a fellow made. Some days I made the enormous sum of 75 cents. Then these rocks were put on the rutty road bed, and farmers, after their crops were laid by, were hired to bring their wagons and haul gravel from the creek and cover up the rocks to settle them down. One evening a wagoner didn't get there until the gravel spreader, who stayed there to spread it, had gone home, causing us to dump it all in one high pile in the middle of the road, and leave it. That very night three boys, going to a watermelon patch, came galloping up the road on horseback, three abreast, the middle one riding a mule. When the mule hit that high pile of gravel, it stood him on his head, throwing the boy off.

Then the mule jumped up, and headed back towards home. His rider yelled at his companions, "Catch him, boys, Papa don't know I slipped him out."

These two on a gray western and a small pony, ran that mule through Shackle Island faster than anything had ever passed through before. They finally caught the mule and Papa never missed the critter. But no melons were stolen that night.

Billy the Goat's
Tales of Two Towns
By L. D. R.

Since everything we read about or see on T.V. these days is something about the Watergate affair, here is a story of an engineering feat involving water that was accomplished near Shackle Island before the Panama Canal was finished. This is also a story about one of my first school teachers who was a very popular man in his district, being a large land owner, a surveyor, notary public and legislator. He was well known and respected all over the county. As a teacher, he had a unique way of keeping perfect order in the one-room school where he taught. If anyone dropped a pin on the floor or made any unnecessary noise he was quick to jump to his feet and lecture all of us about giving us a whaling. However, no one knew exactly what a whaling meant and was afraid to try to find out. One time a group of grown boys slipped off at Noon for a whole week and built a huge dam across St. John Creek, midway between the old turnpike and Happy Hollow Road, which ran parallel for a half-mile and in a few yards on either side of this swimming pool. Then one day after the water cleared up the bell rang after the Noon hour was over and only a half-dozen small boys showed up, causing this honorable teacher to ask if anyone knew where all the rest of the boys were. One little boy piped up and said, "They are up the creek in a washing." Promptly our teacher picked up his walking cane with a cowhorn on the end and declared he would go up and investigate. When he neared, the boys were having a water fight splashing water over each other, knowing that if a buggy or wagon approached they could hear the iron tires on either rocky road and duck down in the water and hide all but their heads. But they never heard their teacher until he looked down on them from the high bank above and shouted, "Well, yes, right here on the public highway in a washing. We are having school down here, I came to invite you in." Before he said the last word, everyone of them had jumped into his clothes and was on his way down the creek to the school house, all expecting a whaling. When our teacher got back all were busy studying and he calmly sat down in his chair and said, "Susie, come up here honey and say your ABC's."

When we small fry grew up into teenagers we had another teacher who was just as distinguished for later he served in Governor Browning's cabinet in the field of education. This teacher sponsored debates between us boys and we held a debate every Friday night that drew a house full of listeners, for at that time there were no radios or telephones in their homes to entertain them. Perhaps it wasn't our feeble efforts to debate that brought them out, but the jokes and stories we told on our opponents which always brought a laugh out of the audience.

For instance one story told was one of these boys got a job during the summer months between school terms at a leading supermarket in Goodlettsville, where you told the clerk what you wanted and he would bring it and stack it on the counter before you. It was too far for this boy to walk from Shackle Island to work and there were no automobiles at that time to commute in, so the merchant roomed and boarded him in his own home, which was beside the railroad track. The first night the boy spent there his boss took him to his room to retire and told him that if he wanted anything during the night to come down the hall to where the merchant slept and call him. The room assigned to the boy happened to be the one nearest the track and he soon went sound asleep, but around midnight a long freight train pulling the grade chugging and puffing woke him up. When he looked out the window he saw great blazes of fire coming out of the smoke stack of the old steam locomotive. Soon the caboose, all brightly lit up, came thundering by scaring him more than ever. Down the hall he ran to the boss' door yelling for the boss to get up. When the merchant came to the door and asked what was wrong, the frightened boy blatted out, "Hell's a moving and two loads done passed by." This brought a roaring laugh from the audience because the setting of the story was true. They knew about where the boy had worked and slept, so it was easy for them to believe the rest of it.

Anyway, this boy had it coming to him for when his opponent, the most oratorical of all of us, got up to speak, this same boy jumped up and introduced him to the audience as having "the voice of a lion and the head of a goat." This way of jumping up unexpectedly when an opponent rose to speak and giving him a joking introduction was an innovation we boys, ourselves, added to give our audience a laugh.

September 13, 1973
Goodlettsville Gazette

Billy the Goat's
Tales of Two Towns
By L. D. R.

The old one armed man who used to work for me on the farm, when told that one of his several nephews had gotten drunk and landed in the Gallatin jail, would always remark, "Yes, they all have to go back home to see the folks."

Fortunately during my long lifetime I have never been sent to jail to see the folks but one time, and that time I was a member of the grand jury and sent there to inspect the place.

However, Sunday afternoon before Labor Day I went to the annual reunion of the great McMurtry clan for the express purpose of seeing the folks and enjoyed the visit very much, meeting all whom I hadn't seen since last year.

History states that John McMurtry, the forerunner of this clan, migrated to Nashville on a boat with James Robertson. Later, after serving as a soldier in the Revolutionary War, he was awarded a land grant near Shackle Island. All who are living today are his great, great, grandchildren and our descendants. However, I wish to pay homage to his wife, whose tomb in Beech Cemetery, I think, says her name was Elizabeth, because she was the one who gave my hometown the name is has been called ever since.

This couple had at least four sons and tradition says that one day a friend came and asked for one of them. She answered, "He has gone courting down at the shack on the island." Now if this son was Wilkke and he married the lady, she was one of my great grandmothers. She was probably the first lady who grew up and got married on this 100 acre island where the dilapidated old flour mill is rotting away today.

Many of the descendants of John McMurtry moved away from this land grant here in the hills to leveler ground, but a few of them stayed. Maybe everyone doesn't know that the highest grave marker in Tennessee or maybe the world is at the foot and head of Uncle Billy McMurtry's grave here in Beech Cemetery. He must have set out two small cedar trees where he wanted to be buried between and there he was buried about three quarters of a century ago. These trees today are nearly a hundred feet high and big enough for saw logs. This man was a preacher and a prophet who predicted the very day of the week he would die and that his second wife would be coming from the barn with a basket of eggs when his cousin Dan got there to lay him out. All of this came true according to this cousin as did Uncle Billy's prediction that men would someday fly through the air like birds. Not only that, but he was the first man in these parts to ever see a flying saucer, although he didn't recognize it by that name.

He was coming from New Hope, where he had preached, one dark night and when he reached the edge of his Granddaddy John's domain he took a short cut through the woods and fields. A bright light started hovering over him. It scared his horse so badly that when they reached the barn lot gate the horse threw Uncle Billy off, crashed the gate, and ran on to the barn.

This same man of the cloth was also a philosopher who took life in its stride, always looking on the bright side of it, as he did when left to be both father and mother to a houseful of children. One little boy had a bad spell of sickness and one day Grandmother Ralph, who was sister of this old times, asked how the little boy was getting along and got this answer. "If he dies, he dies. If he lives he'll be a horse." The boy lived and made a splendid enterprising man who never strayed on the forbidden path but once. That was when he and a neighbor decided to get rich by setting up a still in a nearby empty house by the big spring in a remote spot. The first night at the vacant house, they were getting things ready for a wild catter from the mountains to come by the next night to show them how to get started. However, this fellow decided to come a night earlier and when they saw him coming up the path in the bright moonlight, they thought he was a revenue man coming and they out ran their shoes back over the hill to home. This proves that a good scare will do more good toward making law abiding citizens sometimes than all the laws of the country.

Then there was Cousin Bob of the same generation, who grew up in the hills above Shackle Island and became the village blacksmith making the sparks fly a few years before taking up carpentry and house building where we got better acquainted.

One day I asked him if he ever did any farming and he astounded me with this answer, "No, I have always had to work." Well, I guess it is silly to call farming work, for cultivating ten rows of strawberries with a gooseneck hoe like I have this year is war—fighting weeds and grass that tried to take them.

Cousin Bob, when just a boy, contributed more to humanity and law and order than he ever did in his latter years as you will see when you read the following.

A wily farmer invited Cousin Bob and a friend to come to his house on Saturday night to a chicken supper. He told them to bring two fat hens to cook. When they told him they had no fat hens, he told them to steal a couple. Shortly after dark that night they appeared at the farmer's kitchen with two hens which his wife dressed and cooked. They feasted on chicken and dumplings.

The farmer complimented the boys for such good judgment of fat hens, then asked if they would mind telling him where they got the hens. "We don't mind a bit in the world. We picked them off your chicken roost before we got to your kitchen door," Bob jubilantly informed the schemer.

March 14, 1974
Goodlettsville Gazette

Billy the Goat's Tales of Two Towns By L. D. R.

These days with a crisis in the supply and price of all commodities, the bank of humor is closed until someone cuts another monkey-shine to report. So instead of laughable matter it's a write up about towns and places past and present around Vertical Plains visited occasionally in my lifetime.

At four o'clock Wednesday afternoon we hitched a ride to Stone Wall Jackson's retreat, a modern mansion back in a woodland pasture, for supper and also a visit with our oldest daughter, Carleen, who, thanks, is much better. On our way up there we stopped at a store in Shackle Island across the creek from the big island from which the town gets its name. We bought a can of salmon for one dollar and seventy five cents, which used to cost fifteen cents or two for a quarter. High priced eating.

It is considered ill manners to eat and run but that is what we did because our host, who brought us home with them, had to be at a songfest at six o'clock, but thank goodness they could not run more than 55 miles an hour and we enjoyed the trip and supper too. Going and coming back we passed through a ghost town, now a wilderness, that in bygone days was Tyree Springs summer resort, where two Presidents and several Governors spent vacations drinking the healthy sulphur water around the spacious hotel. That hotel is now completely gone and a first class highway up the hill runs right across where the hotel stood.

We also passed through White House, which still retains its old stage coach name. Who knows if it was so named for a house painted white or from one where a man named White lived.

Funny thing, once while doing carpenter work at a garage in Goodlettsville, a stranger hung around there all day having his car worked on and I thought he was a tourist passing through. I asked where he was from and he answered White House. I said your name is Jones, I suppose and in astonishment he said yes and asked how I knew. Not too long after that I was sitting in my car in front of a doctor's office and another man was in his car waiting like I was for a patient to come out and I asked where he lived and he, too, answered White House. Again, I said your name must be Jones and quickly he said that is right but how did you know? The Millersville stage coach stop was a man's store whose name I can't recall, but anyway a revenue man named Miller often stopped to eat a lunch and feed his horse. When the moonshiners in upper Sumner County killed the revenue man and hid his body in an old hand-dug well, the name of this stopping place was changed to Millersville.

Us older ones can well remember the big rambling frame house that stood where the Bank of Goodlettsville is today, which was PinHook Inn. It was a stage coach stop until a man named Goodlett built the first super market in this town and its name was changed to Goodlettsville, while its first settler Casper Mansker only had the creek that is the dividing line between Davidson and Sumner counties named after him.

The town of Hendersonville, though, had the most enchanting names when I was a boy and marketed strawberries there. The names of citizens living there that I heard spoken made me think war was going on, such names as Ben Hurt, John Shute, Will Fite. One name though that I heard some of his kin call would carry a letter anywhere in the world, it was Uncle Sam Stamps. To make you think there are forests around the place instead of so much water like there is today there Woods and Groves were often mentioned. If a magistrates' trial was held there in the middle of winter, I imagine all contestants stayed warm if it was held before my best strawberry customer, Squire Summers, who bought nine six-gallon crates from me one day to make pies to feed the Interurban hands at his restaurant.

Then a lady still lives there today who told my daughter she reads this column. Thank you, lady. We all enjoy picking your name out of our gardens and pastures every Spring and Summer.

In the telephone directory there are still lots of Hendersons listed, so there is no reason to ever change the name of this town.

The man best remembered by us old timers in these parts was a big farmer a hundred years ago who raised corn and stored it in a big log corn crib. When he kept missing corn that someone was pulling out through a crack between the logs, he set a steel trap inside on the corn. The next morning when he went to the barn to feed his stock there was a man standing by the crib with his hand stuck in the crack.

This farmer spoke to the thief cordially calling him by his name, then went on and fed his stock. When he came back he told the victim of his trap that breakfast was ready and to come with him to the house to eat. Finally, the poor fellow said, "You know I can't get loose from here." Then the kind-hearted farmer released the hand in the trap, escorted the fellow to the house, had him eat breakfast and then filled his sack full of corn and sent him home.

July 25, 1974
Goodlettsville Gazette

Billy the Goat's
Tales of Two Towns
By L. D. R.

The two towns mentioned above are Goodlettsville and Shackle Island, that have been on the map since pioneer days. But in my boyhood days I witnessed a new town grow up along the pike about halfway between these older towns which in its heyday had more daily action going on there than either of the other two.

Back then it was horse and buggy days for an automobile was yet to be invented and Shackle Island had only a big flour mill which delivered flour and meal to several counties in a big wagon pulled by three big mules hitched side by side. Goodlettsville at that time had only a small copper shop that bought hoop poles to make hoops to go around the flour barrels they made for mills to fill with flour.

This town first started when Aunt Sis and her husband, a railroader, bought a hill farm in Long Hollow and built a two-story house on it a half dozen steps from the old turnpike and also built a barn on it and began raising horses, cattle and hogs. Unfortunately, this new farmer didn't live but a short time, and his widow met and married a Dutchman named Beemer, whom she brought to the farm and ordered to clean up the farm with a grubbing hoe and chopping axe. She also gave him the task of caring for the stock.

This done she went back to Nashville to stay, leaving the Dutchman to do his own cooking in the lean-to kitchen at the back of the high building where he slept in a bed with her two dogs for companionship.

When anyone paid the old fellow a friendly visit he would tell them, "She married me, I never married her," which was absolutely true because he was a Yankee soldier who had been hired to come across the ocean and fight for the Union and consequently drew a fat Federal pension.

Then the greatest boom, ever, started just over the fence from the Dutchman's barn. Two saw mills moved in and began operating on the adjoining wooded hills and two more houses were hastily built to house the mill hands and timber cutters. One mill sawed lumber and cross ties, while the other sawed out hickory spokes for wagons and also for automobiles, like the first cars used when cars were soon to appear in these parts with wooden spokes. This new mushrooming town we called Beemerville.

The sawmill engine had a wildcat whistle on it and the spoke mill engine a steamboat whistle. When these two blew for noon or quitting time, the sound of the two reverberated through these hills as nothing ever had before or since, as I well remember.

Everything was running smoothly until one morning the mill hands found Beemer bad off sick in his lean-to hovel and called the doctor, who pronounced it pneumonia and ordered the front room door opened and the old fellow put in Aunt Sis' fine featherbed where he had never been before. There the neighbors nursed him back to health for no one knew where to call his "loving wife."

Then it came time for the pension check to come and out she came to be there when it was cashed, but the fat was in the fire when she learned the lock had been broken and Beemer had been put in her featherbed.

She became so furious she rushed out to find someone to vent her fury on and found Lena, the wife of one of the mill hands, picking up kindling around the spoke mill and began on her. But Lena was in no mood to listen to such ravings and shoved the furious old lady down on the sawdust and began spanking her with a hickory lathe from a spoke. Aunt Sis began screaming, "Beemer, Beemer, help I am weak." Hearing her screaming for help, he picked up his water bucket and lit out down the pike to the well a half mile away, bursting his sides laughing and saying to everyone he met, "Ooh, I tell you Lena is giving her a good one."

The consequence of this fracas was Lena was arrested and trial was held next day on the front porch of this two story-house.

Squire G. W. Jackson was the one who convened the court there that day and fined Lena $10 while about fifty men and boys stood in the pike listening. Then a hat was passed around through the crowd and $20 made up. The fine was paid and the other $10 was given to Lena to do the job over if she ever had to.

This old building stood there for many years and many humorous things happened there to its tenants, including my wife and I, where we lived the first year of our marriage. All these buildings have been torn down with the last one burning to the ground this last Spring and Beemerville is now a ghost town with nothing left but humorous and startling memories of it, which this column may relate sometime if you care to hear them.

November 7, 1974
Goodlettsville Gazette

Billy the Goat's
Tales of Two Towns
By L. D. R.

The worst thing about living is not getting old and decrepit for that is only a physical problem. The worst thing is not having a host of older friends to fraternize with and listen to them talk.

When the first rural route came through Long Hollow, Grandpa's was one of the first daily papers received. I read all the sensational headlined articles in it, then after supper went down to a near neighbor's, who also got the paper, to listen to his version of these stories without letting him know I had already read it. One day the paper told about Coleman Younger, a famous train robber being released from a Minnesota penitentiary after serving 20 years. This talkative neighbor began spilling out the whole story to me in every detail.

Finally, I asked him how many Younger brother were in the gang and he told me there were four of them. I asked what their names were, which I already knew but wanted to see how well this old timer could remember what he read that day. He began telling me their names by saying, "Let's see, there was Bob Coleman and Jim Coleman and Frank Coleman and there was another one of these I can't think of his name."

"Coleman Coleman," I suggested, and he answered, "That's it Coleman Coleman was the other one." We all started laughing and someone told him that he started out talking about the Younger brothers and now he was calling them Coleman and that was why we were all laughing.

Back at the beginning of this century when I was ten years old there were people who got hungry back then, even though three cans of most everything in the store could be bought for a quarter.

Here is a dialogue I heard at that time and I recall it as well as if it occurred yesterday because my brother and I used to repeat it in the presence of our daddy with all the actions in it.

White whiskered Tom Smith with his wife and a large family of children lived in a log cabin up Lick Hollow, a mile from the old turnpike. One morning he came walking down the pike and said to our daddy, "Johnny by goney I didn't have a bit of bread for breakfast this morning." Daddy threw his hand over his ear and answered, "What say, Tom?" Happily, this old fellow's family didn't go hungry too long for he was on his way to the next house where his sister lived who married a Yankee soldier who drew a fat Federal pension, making her able to help him. Usually Tom had his wife call her brother for help but evidently he got tired of being called to help them, because the boys in the family, whom I went to school with, told this story. Their mother had sent for her brother for help and when he arrived at their cabin and Tom greeted him with "Hello, Amos," and his brother-in-law shouted back, "Hell High."

Up to date news is that the greatest commandment of 1974 has been strictly obeyed here at Vertical Plains as well as elsewhere, which is "Come little leaves said the wind one day. Come out over the yard with me and play. Put on your garments of silver and gold, Summer has gone and Winter is cold." However it is not cold yet and let's hope it doesn't get that way because Mother Nature, who made the wind blow last March to pump the sap up in the trees that caused the leaves to grow on the trees, is not going to help us rake the leaves off our yards and that job we will have to do ourselves if it's done.

Halloween is over and we beat the record for having a trick or treat guest. This time our first one was a hundred and six year old man, who picked up a full grown man as if he were a baby just to show that he himself was still much of a man.

Then someone began pounding on the screen door, which wasn't locked, and I yelled "scratch under," but when the pounding didn't stop I opened the door and it was a tiny little boy lacking six weeks being a year old and just learning to walk. That was all the guests we had that night, but some mugwump shot off a whole pack of firecrackers in our mailbox. Next time I will have a foot tub full of water in the tree above the box, that will douse him when he opens the mail box door.

Here is a modern proverb: "Blessed is he who expecteth nothing for in that he shall not be deceived." However, he may get a big surprise, like for instance, we sent our new neighbors, whom we had never met, a pumpkin for Halloween, expecting nothing in return. But instead, the lady cooked the pumpkin and made pies out of it, and that very day she brought us a delicious pie to eat, while we waited up for the gang of prowlers to show up.

Thank you, Mrs. Duncan, you chose a good and practical way to get real good out of pumpkin on Halloween.

November 28, 1974
Goodlettsville Gazette

Billy the Goat's
Tales of Two Towns
By L. D. R.

"More rain—more rest," used to be a welcome slogan in past years, but what we need today is to all start singing, "T'aint goner rain no more, no more." Maybe the ordinance they once passed in Nashville making it against the law to sing that song, they will no longer try to enforce. When the weatherman predicted last night a twenty percent chance of showers this afternoon, he must have meant that much chance of sunshine, for the rain poured down all the morning and the sun has popped out a minute or two this afternoon.

I never knew but one weather forecaster and he predicted the weather in such unique language that you never left confused. It was May 1919 and we were setting tobacco after a good rain the day before. The sun was shining brightly with two or three white clouds around the horizon that looked like snow covered mountains. This fellow stopped setting tobacco a moment and raised up, looked around and said, "It's liable to rain today, liable not." Now had that fellow been around this year, he would have hit the nail on the head most any day he made such a prediction.

Well, of all things, here is something you and I, nor no one else ever heard tell of before, nearly a week before the story about possum hunting came out in this column, two boys from town drove in here after dark to go possum hunting. They said they didn't have a dog with them, but were going to try to catch them with a flashlight, leaving me still wondering if these boys had been listening to Grandpa on TV tell about Trailblazer dog food having hunting power and had been eating the stuff.

Anyway, I was disappointed, because I was too decrepit to try to beat them to the top of the hill by going another way, to scream like a wild cat to rush them back to the house with something to tell. Mother Nature soon ran then out of the woods with a shower of rain and these two had nothing exciting to tell about their hunt. This was unlike it was when I was their age and got scared out of the woods or scared someone else.

The first time to ever go hunting, three of us small boys started up a long wooded hollow and the leaves on ahead of us began to rattle loudly. Our dogs cowered behind us when we tried to sic them on whatever it was rattling the leaves.

Every time we moved forward with our lantern, we found nothing, but the noise would start again the same distance ahead of us. We got scared and ran home telling such a scary tale that Grandpa and Uncle Stephen rushed back with us to the spot. Everything was still as a mouse. This has been a mystery ever since as to whether it was somebody pranking with us or a fierce wild animal our dogs were afraid to tackle. A few years later when my brother and I were grown, we were out hunting on the high ridge at the head of this same deep hollow and heard voices talking down in it which we recognized as the voices of two elderly men, Mitch Cantrel and Jimmy Hullet. Then while my brother hid our lantern, I ran around through the dry leaves screaming like a wildcat and their dogs headed for home yelping like they had been beaten with a limb. Mitch yelled out, "That's that damn wolf" as both of them fired their muzzle loading shot, falling far below me. They had both fired both barrels of their old guns and. knowing it would take several minutes to reload them, I screamed again as I ran straight toward them and they took out after their dogs yelling, "Here, here," trying to call them back. As they ran they put caps on their guns and fired them to make noise. The next day it was all over the county that a wolf had run them out of the woods.

A couple of years later a wolf killed a sheep one snowy night and Old Casey, a sheep dog, chased him all day until the sheep killer crawled in a hollow log and bit one hunter's hand when the hunter tried to pull him out By shooting in the log they ended the wolf scare in this neck of the woods.

January 16, 1975
Goodlettsville Gazette

Billy the Goat's
Tales of Two Towns
By L. D. R.

New Year's Day 1975—and I only remember two such days in the past, and they both proved to be very disastrous for me. On this day in 1914, the weather was nice and warm like it is this time and I started that morning cleaning up a rich new ground of virgin soil to raise my first crop of burley tobacco.

I had a man hired to help me and my brother came along and decided to go in with me on the project. We three cut logs to get lumber to build a barn to house the tobacco and harvested the finest crop of weeds that has ever been grown around Shackle Island. With tobacco selling that Fall for 30 cents per pound, we had three thousand pounds and sold it on the Gallatin market for a hundred and twenty dollars, because it houseburned in the barn. Who could forget a misfortune like that even though it had a bright side to it, for experience is the best teacher. We learned how to take care of all other crops we have grown since.

The year before on New Year's Day 1913, when I was twenty two years old, we went rabbit hunting on the broad expanse of the western plains that was grown up in tall cactus and cedars with all kinds of undergrowth and we became completely lost. When we started out Pikes Peak, covered with snow, was directly behind us and we thought all we had to do was return toward it, but after we hunted until we were hungry and thirsty, we discovered that there were snow covered peaks on all sides of us. The teenage boy with me and I were completely lost.

We came to a clearing in the wilderness with a ranch house occupied by two bachelors who knew me as the store clerk where they traded. They had us stay and eat dinner with them after we had gotten a drink at the windmill from a well 1400 feet deep.

They had no blackeyed peas for dinner that day, but we had excellent luck finding our way back home after they showed us which one was Pikes Peak. The only way anyone can hope to get any luck out of blackeyed peas is to feed them to the chickens to make them lay, then eat the eggs which you can digest easily and they won't leave you miserable for a whole week afterward.

This New Year's Day our youngest son, Wallace, and all his family went hiking in the deep forest of Long Hollow. If they had become lost they would have had a great surprise and found out where they were when they climbed to the top of Joyner's Knob and looked away down below them. They would have seen the busy city of Goodlettsville and ten miles further away, the skyscrapers of Nashville, then turned around and looked down at Shackle Island and at Gallatin another ten miles away.

In the days of my youth, and probably a century before then, the fertile fields around the base of this high knob were growing corn and other farm crops. Today most of them are grown up in briars and small trees. There were also a half dozen houses around this base. One of them, a big log structure, was Jones' Chapel, where I first went to Sunday School and preaching before the present building was erected further down the valley, and all of them are gone today except one.

One of them was gone before my day. It was the closest to the knob, where some time after the Civil War a former slave named Joyner acquired a few acres and built a house on it. Later, when my Daddy bought it from him, only the fallen chimney was there. Here on this very tract of land, I first saw corn planted when I was three or four years old, but I still remember it. After riding in the two-horse wagon a mile or more to this remote spot, a grown young lady baby sitter guarded my younger brother and me under a nearby mulberry tree to keep us from getting snake bit, while our Mother dropped the corn for Daddy to cover with the plow that laid off the rows.

When these New Year's hikers descended from this lofty knob, they visited the house that was left and it was vacant. It had been vacant for years because the place was spooky. No one ever lived in it any length of time because of the strange thing that occurred every day at twelve Noon. The last fellow who bought this farm and house had it surveyed. When the surveyor and his helpers got all the way around it, he sat down to figure up the acreage in front of the house. As the Shackle Island Flour Mill stopped blowing for Noon, something that sounded like a big black dog came crashing down through the limbs of a tall beech tree near there and hit the ground with a loud thump. When they ran to see what it was, they found nothing nor no sign that anything had hit the ground.

If this mysterious phenomenon was ever solved there is no record of it.

May 1, 1975
Goodlettsville Gazette

**Billy the Goat's
Tales of Two Towns
By L. D. R.**

Maybe you know and maybe you don't, that "maybe" day comes each year, just thirty days after April Fool's Day, so herein lies a story.

The year I was 21, I was working in Nashville and boarding there. On April Fool's Day I received a long love letter from a lovesick lady. I concluded she lived near Shackle Island where all the girls live whom I grew up with, but I had no idea which one she was. That letter was outstanding for the many times she told me how much she loved me. It was signed, "The lovingest girl for you in the wide, wide world."

The next April I was back home in Long Hollow and here came another April Fool addressed to me there. It was similar to the first one, only she grumbled a lot because I hadn't answered the first letter she sent me. It was signed, "As long as the vine runs round the stump, I'll be your darling sugar lump." This lady must have kept track of me pretty well for the next April I was working in Kansas City and I received the third note from her and it was signed, "The Mysterious Ghost," which did it for me, being made a monkey of, whoever she was.

All these letters were postmarked Hendersonville. So, I sent this last letter and the contents to the Shackle Island carrier to see if he could remember whose box he got it from so he could deliver an answer to it there. He answered back, saying he could, but didn't say whose box it was, which I didn't want to know. So I wrote this April Fool sender a three page letter that began, "Maybe."—"Maybe I

know who you are or maybe I don't. Maybe you are the apple of my eye or maybe you are the thorn in my eye." I continued with every silly "Maybe" I could think of then signed it "A Simple-headed Sap."

The letter I addressed to Miss Terious Ghost. That did the job, for I never got another April Fool from her and never learned who she was and never think about her except around the first of May. I don't give a hoot now who she might have been.

Four years later, when I was 25 a pretty little lady who was not even a teenager and had never heard of me when these silly letters started coming, happened to be out scouting one afternoon and stumbled over me and forthwith adopted me as her lifelong protector and provider. I have been her slave ever since, so why should I worry about any lost love.

When I was a teenager, I dated maybe a half dozen nice girls, but the first one I dated almost cost me my life. I was working for a farmer helping get in his crops and this farmer had a young daughter who had never dated anyone. One faint hearted youngster asked me to make a date with her for him to bring her out to church a certain night, but I would have felt like a fool had I made a date with her for another fellow. I owned a horse and a new rubber tired buggy, so consequently I escorted her to church that night.

A week after the protracted meeting was over, a big party was given for the young folks out on the highway to which I brought her from her home a mile out on a side road with a gate that had to be opened then shut to get to her home. Leaving her on her front porch, I immediately got in my buggy and started for home, but when halfway to the gate two fellows stepped out of the darkness and stopped my horse. They told me that the young fellow whom I had double-crossed with the girl had organized a wild mob and had wired the gate and was waiting on the bluff to rock me. They then opened a gate into a farmer's barn lot and

187

we drove to another gate onto the highway a half mile from where the mob was waiting for me, all of them jealous because I had been with the girl.

Later, I learned this mob waited for me until way after twelve o'clock then got scared that they would get into trouble if they left the gate wired up on a country road. However, they never once considered the fact that if there were a David in that mob, he might have killed me and caused my horse to whirl around with my buggy and tear it to pieces and get hurt too. Anyway, the joke was on them, for they had that gate so securely wired with barbed wire twisted so tightly with the wire pliers, that it took them until two o'clock to get the gate unwired and them on their way home.

That was one night that my two friends were really friends indeed.

July 10, 1975
Goodlettsville Gazette

**Billy the Goat's
Tales of Two Towns
By L. D. R.**

I must clear up something that was in last week's column. My good friend Jee O'Saile, who comes by sometimes and helps me do some manual labor that I'm unable to do myself, wants to know where Barely Do is. The settlement mentioned last week. Well sir, it is midway between Grab All in Sumner County and Dog Town in Robertson County, and only a few miles south of Scatterville. To get there you go north on 31W, past all the firecracker stands, until you cross Honey Run Creek. Then go another mile and turn off on a road to the right, which will take you by Bottle Top Filling Station, where I once stopped to get some air in a tire. When the lady clerk learned who I was she exclaimed, "So you're the one who writes that column in the GOODLETTSVILLE GAZETTE! That being the case I'll have to charge you for the air you put in that tire." The she laughed a big laugh. I answered, "That's perfectly all right as long as you charge it." But to this day I've never received a statement and can't report how much a pound they sold air at that time at Bottle Top Stop. This was a name I gave the store myself in referring to it in this column, because all the tops off cold drink bottles that had been opened there for years had been thrown out around the gas pumps and front porch making for smoother driving than gravel would have made, and also a perfect advertisement for cold drinks.

Barely Do is a few miles further out the road, and how it got its name I do not know, but I hope some reader will let us know why it was ever given such a name.

A few days ago the question was asked, "What Tennessean was awarded the Nobel Peace Prize?" The answer was Cordell Hull. Perhaps some of you never heard how this famous man got started on the road to fame or what caused him to be elected to Congress the first time he ran for such an office The incumbent Congressman he ran against was E. E. Miller, and the Seventh (or Shackle Island) District of Sumner County was for Miller. But one night Miller came to this little crossroads voting place in the back of a store. The place was crowded with voters all over the store, some sitting on counters and chairs, but most standing. About the time Miller was in the middle of his speech-making of pleas and promises, a nail keg that a farmer was sitting on turned over with him and he went sprawling out onto the floor, causing a big uproar of laughter. But instead of Miller laughing with them, he got as mad as a wet hen and proceeded to give the farmer a genuine bawling out for being so clumsy and interrupting his speech.

This turned the tide, for the voters couldn't stand a man who couldn't laugh with them over something that happened purely by accident. When the votes were counted, the two men were running neck to neck until the Shackle Island votes came in with 350 for Hull that would have gone for Miller if he had held his temper. Moral: This shows that getting mad sometimes and losing your temper will do you a lot more harm than good.

I am glad to report that I was able to attend the Old Beech Homecoming July 6, where I enjoyed meeting many old friends and acquaintants. My old schoolmate and friend Irby Hutchison came up to me and said he'd heard that I had been sick, but he didn't come to see me. I answered, "You needn't have told me that, for I already knew you didn't come to see me," getting a laugh out of the bystanders.

July 17, 1975
Goodlettsville Gazette

Billy the Goat's
Tales of Two Towns
By L. D. R.

This year the price of peaches has skyrocketed. The week I was in the hospital, Wallace, our youngest son, went out driving around to buy a few to eat. He stopped at Cousin Frank Redding's, a leading orchardist around Union Hill and also a fellow as full of fun as a dog is fleas. Wallace was dumbfounded when this joker began asking about me and calling me Cousin Luther, which as most of you know, is my given name. Wallace came back telling me he didn't know I was any kin to

Frank Redding, so here is how we came to be kin:

Frank's mother and Burford Rice's mother are sisters, and one day we went over to visit Burford and there on the front porch with him sat Sam Redding, Frank's older brother who was the same age as I was. He didn't know me from Adam's off-ox, but I recognized him and after shaking hands with Burford, I walked over and shook hands with Sam saying, "Hello, Cousin Sam, how are you?" and he was dumbfounded, until I told him I was just mocking his cousin, Smokey Redding, our neighbor who called him that so many times when telling me about him. This amused Frank so much he started calling me Cousin Luther, and me calling him Cousin Frank.

At the time this occurred and long before this, I ran a carpenter shop for a brother of Frank's wife, and that is when I first met and got acquainted with Frank. When we met out on the street or anywhere else we would speak to each other, then he would ask me to loan him two dollars. Knowing he had more money than Carter had oats, I knew he was only kidding. But one time we happened to be where a large crowd had assembled, and I walked by him when he was talking to three or four friends of his and mine, too, and to make them laugh he stopped me and said, "Loan me two dollars." I handed him a two-dollar bill, which he looked at and handed back to me, saying, "I've got two of them in my pocket now."

This all happened a few years ago, but last Saturday afternoon we stopped at Cousin Frank's and I was much disappointed because we couldn't find hair nor hide of him anywhere. I had stopped to buy two dollars' worth of peaches to see how full he'd fill a gallon basket.

My most outstanding get well message (and I am mighty grateful for all of 'em) I'm sorry I didn't get until I got back home. It was sent to the hospital first and forwarded on to Vertical Plains. In large black letters it showed it was from the Springfield Chamber of Commerce, and in much larger letters in blue ink it was addressed to me at Baptist Hospital. Had I gotten this before I left the hospital I could have shown it to all the nurses and attendants, and I would have made them think I was some punkin.

At the homecoming Sunday at Old Beech I met a lady there I hadn't seen in more than 65 years, and I didn't even know she was still living She was 92 years old, and I was very much embarrassed talking to here because I was afraid she would think I was the one that stole the popcorn balls from her house one night when she was having a dance The joke about the whole thing was that there was another lady at the dance and there was this fellow who was courting her daughter who had told him to find out who stole the candy. But all he did was to ask us boys to start smoking cigarettes or something to keep anybody from smelling the candy on our breath. What this lady didn't know was that he was the fictitious "J. Proctor Knott," founder and president of the Shackle Island Board of Health. He would have been the last one to spill the beans about who took the candy, even if he had known for sure. The large platter of popcorn balls was on the kitchen table, and the kitchen door securely locked, but what they failed to do was blow out the light in the oil lamp, making the candy a tempting bait from the outside window, which one of the rascals held up while another one crawled through to get the candy,

Of course, I was as guilty as any of the rest of them because I ate a ball or two of the candy when all of us were called out into the yard. We then took the platter with the remainder of the candy, and placed it on the seat of a two horse wagon. When the wagon riders started back home, they found the candy there. Thanks to Ms. Callie Taylor, with a plea for forgiveness, for the candy we ate. I wish her many more years of candy making without fear, for the few survivors left are far too old to be prowling around.

July 24, 1975
Goodlettsville Gazette

Billy the Goat's Tales of Two Towns By L. D. R.

I'm in the dog house now and have been since yesterday when I was accused of embarrassing my family because I steadfastly refused to comply with the false god of style that is an epidemic in this country today. Yesterday, the mayor of Goshentown brought a young photographer to Vertical Plains to take our picture to store away in the archives of Old Beech Church for future generations to look at. I had my hat on my head when several pictures were taken of us. I wanted future generations to know that hats were worn by all old timers in bygone days.

It was only a few years ago when one of the Jones boys stood around bareheaded causing us older ones to think he was a maniac, as crazy as a bat. But the younger boys, like a flock of sheep when the leader jumps through a hole in the fence they all follow after, tried to keep up with the Joneses, and now many of the older ones are dong the same.

Our hats were the only means we had of showing respect. On entering a church we took them off and placed them in a hat rack, and riding on an elevator, we held them in our hands if ladies were on it. We tipped to ladies we met in buggies or elsewhere, while to men we merely bowed or threw up our hand. One day this week we saw on the front page of our paper another one of the Jones boys, who was once the President of the United States, walking along the beach of California stone barefooted Now, I'm waiting to see how many that voted for him will start going barefooted, too.

Here is the other half of what happened this week that gave me the biggest scare I ever had in my whole life: Our son, driving up the highway to visit us, spied a truck parked in the cow pasture and told us he was going back down there to find out if it was thieves in the orchard stealing plums and peaches He stayed gone so long I became terribly afraid he had confronted a gang in the orchard that had knocked him in the head and, to destroy the evidence against them, had fled in the truck. But what had happened, he had parked his own car in the gate so that this suspicious truck couldn't get out. Then he waited for the pilferers to come back to their truck to find out who they were and what they were after.

Of course, I knew nothing about that and couldn't get any of the neighbors over the phone to go down there with me to investigate because none of them were home to answer, or they would have come running. It was too far for me to try to walk, but, thankfully, all my fears and worry were for nothing, because it was an old man and his wife out picking some dried up blackberries. They should have parked their truck in our yard and told us what they were doing.

Last night a truck load of our offspring and some friends, left here at almost sundown to go to the orchard to gather what was left of the plums and peaches, After they left I happened to think that I should have given them a twist of tobacco to have with them in case one of them got stung by a bumblebee or yellow jacket. Sure enough, just after dark here came two of the grandsons rushing in the truck to get some tobacco to draw out the poison of a sting on the leg of one of granddaughter Sharon's girl friends. That gave me another worry because they didn't have the tobacco to put on the sting a lot sooner, but it gave her relief anyway.

Now a last word about hats: The most outstanding man in the United States in 1974 made the front page of the daily paper wearing a hat on his head. He was a young fellow, only 21, who was the proud father of quintuplets, so if he wears a hat so young, I feel it's entirely proper for me, exactly 4 times his age, to wear one, too. So if any of my guardians who claim that my pictures wearing a hat for posterity will embarrass them, they should applaud it or else my ghost wearing hat might haunt them the rest of their lives.

October 16, 1975
Gazette & Star News

Billy the Goat's
Tales of Two Towns
By L. D R.

When I was twenty five years old, my life had been fraught with so many dangers I didn't think it could last much longer. Then one night a pretty young lady stopped in the house I was remodeling, after being called in by the two spinster ladies I was working for. I made my first date with her to bring her on to church where she had started. This was the first date I had made with a girl since I was a teenager. I fell in love with her that very night. However, I courted her about 18 months before we were married, to make sure she wasn't double crossing me by having a date with someone else. I knew that a pretty thing like her could have dated a dozen others had she chose to, but fortunately she didn't choose to.

When I was a teenager I had many close calls, but had been spared for some reason. Like the time another boy and I walked up to where some timber cutters were cutting a large oak tree. When I looked up, the tree was coming down right on top of me and I was scared so badly I couldn't move, which was all that saved my life, for when it hit the ground I was standing right in the forks of it with a big saw log on each side of me and never got a scratch. Another time I was sent to a neighbor's by my grandmother to get milk and butter. When I arrived home and started to get off my horse, my foot slipped out from under me, leaving my other foot hung in the stirrup and the horse running, dragging me, but luckily the horse kicked me on the hip and jarred my foot out of the stirrup and kept from dragging me to death.

However, the nearest I ever came to getting killed I was working for a farmer and a faint hearted young fellow wanted me to make a date for him with the farmer's young daughter. I would have felt like a heel had I done so instead of making the date for myself, so when I did and brought her out to a party this young rascal organized a mob to wire up the gate on the county road after I had carried her home, than rock me when I got out of my buggy to open it. Fortunately two friends overheard his diabolical plan and met me halfway to the gate and led me by a barn lot and on to the highway a nearer way, leaving this mob to wait for me a couple of hours, then unwire the gate themselves, because they were afraid to leave it wired up on a county road.

The next narrow escape I had was out in the wild and wooly west. I started to walk across a rye patch along the banks of Turkey Creek and a young red cow grazing on this rye came charging after me with her head lowered to gore me with her long horns. How I managed to jump back over this barbed wire fence with a rabbit in one hand and my shotgun in the other, I'll never know, but I did and saved my life.

The next episode I had was far removed from here, along the Heirfano River a hundred miles south of Turkey Creek. I started work one Sunday afternoon under Mr. Hardy, the civil engineer on the job. I never worked for a better boss in my whole life. I worked that afternoon and all the next day and he found no fault with me. The next day though the black bearded young straw-boss took over. I had heard the hands tell how mean he was.

The next morning when I went to work down in the muddy reservoir we were working on the day before, he walked by me and yelled, "Do about down there, Slim. Let that shovel work a little faster," which made me mad as a hornet for I was doing my best. Then an hour or so later, he came back and

195

yelled, "You'll have to work a little faster, Slim!" This was more than I could take and I brought the shovel up over my shoulder and stuck it in the mud behind me and yelled, "I don't have to do anything but die. If you don't like the way I work give me my time and I'll quit." Then I whirled and faced him holding both hands near my pockets like I was ready to shoot him and he wilted down. I had no gun in my pocket, but he probably thought I had, and said meekly, "If you want your time go tell Mr. Hardy." I promptly did. When I got back to the tent I heard the cooks laughing about how I had bluffed that mean straw-boss that they all hated. Mr. Hardy paid me what was coming to me without saying a word. Then I had to walk several miles back to the depot, while great herds of cattle stood and gazed at me, but none of them started toward me When I reached the depot, there was a train going the other way and the conductor of the freight train told me if I was aiming to ride that train to get in the caboose, but I thanked him and told him I was going the other way. Arriving back in Pueblo, I caught a train for Kansas City and forgot the wild and wooly West. Thirty years later I visited Stone City with my wife and it was nothing but a ghost town with all the buildings gone except a post office that mail reached twice a week.

February 18, 1976
Gazette & Star

Billy the Goat's Tales of Two Towns By L. D. Ralph

Today reminds me of a day many years ago when I was able to prowl these wooded hills. I was up on the side of one of them overlooking the highway and heard a buggy traveling down the road. It was Perpetual Smiler going to Goodlettsville with a buggy load of sweet potatoes to sell to the merchants there.

Then, hearing a noise overhead, I looked up and saw three single passenger airplanes flying low over the treetops, and I realized a great change had occurred in the world. These planes were, perhaps, out searching for a wildcat still, but found none, because there are no everlasting springs in these hills, which they didn't know.

In the long ago a Yankee soldier put on a show to try to gain possession of part of these hills, but he made a failure with his diabolic plan. His plan was to get his mother-in-law to give his wife a certain portion of her property, which almost ran this old lady crazy and stirred up the neighborhood for miles around. He would call on a spirit to knock on a wall three times if it wanted his wife to be given the peach orchard hollow portion of the property, and there were always three knocks on the wall, just as he planned

Finally, a mob went in one night and took the old fellow out and gave him a whipping, and he had several men arrested. There was a big trial in Gallatin, but these men were too smart for him. They had stayed at home that night and had sent their sons to do the whipping, which he didn't know.

At the trial this old man named one man whom he called "Fiesty Bill" who he said was one of the group that whipped him. He declared he would know the fellow's voice in hell. That fellow proved by his wife that he was at home that night, and all the others he accused did likewise, so all of them were cleared, and the old fellow never did get possession of that property.

Years later my father bought this property that the old conniver tried so hard to get, and on it I had several experiences. I shall never forget one night while out coon hunting, my dogs began barking at a half grown polecat on the ground. I picked up the polecat by the nap of its neck to bring home to make a pet out of it, knowing these animals can't spray their obnoxious scent unless their feet are on the ground But when I got home and put the little varmint in a coop where I could feed it, I failed to pull my hand back out of the coop quick enough after releasing the varmint. It bit my hand with its sharp teeth My thumb became very sore and this taught me never again to try to make a pet out of a wild animal, which was a good lesson to learn.

A few years later I was picking up some tobacco sticks and sharpening them and had them about sharpened when Uncle George, who had a mortal fear of snakes, yelled, "Whoop! Look at that copperhead!" "Where do you see a snake?" I asked him. He told me right under the few sticks left, where I had been picking up from a pile on a log. I hit at the snake and saw where two of them were coiled together, which unnerved me, and I told him to kill the snakes, which he did.

April 28, 1976
Gazette & Star

Billy the Goat's Tales of Two Towns By L. D. Ralph

L. E. Graves on Campbell Road sent me word that he liked last week's article written from this hospital dungeon, so I'll try to please him again. I understand that Mr. Graves has been a storekeeper for many years and just retired from clerking at Reid's Market. He probably knows a lot of wild tales he could tell me, like being robbed at gunpoint a few times.

When I clerked at the General Store not far from Pueblo more than 60 years ago, we heard of a dance to be held Friday night at the school house, and the boss said we would close the store and go up there. We did go, and while the boss and Mayor Kelley were standing there with me watching the dance, they decided they wanted me to get out on the floor and dance. I told them I couldn't, but they said Mrs. Kelley, the Mayor's wife, would teach me. She was a nice old lady who came into the store often.

Finally, I got up the nerve to go over and say, "Mrs. Kelley, would you teach me how to dance?" She quickly replied, "Why sure, Mr. Ralph, with pleasure." I believe she meant it, too. Out on the floor she started swinging me 'round and 'round. And then another woman would grab me and swing me the same, until I was getting so dizzy I didn't know what I was doing When they finally turned me loose, I was as drunk as a boiled owl, but I managed to stagger to the wall without falling. They, of course, all had a big laugh out of me. That's the way they initiated me, and I'm sure Mrs. Kelley must have winked at all those gray haired ladies and had them in on the joke.

They all simply made a monkey out of me and gave me enough dancing to last a lifetime,

Another time a team came out from Pueblo to initiate some of us into the Woodmen Of The World. We had to stand on the outside until they told us to come in. There was one old man out there and some drunk fellows. The drunks got around the old man and told him he was to be the one to ride the goat. This scared the old man to death, and finally the organizer came outside and told the drunks to leave the old man alone. He said if they didn't he'd see that everyone of them would have to ride the cactus bushes back to Pueblo. I think the organizer meant to sic all of us fellows that were to be initiated on those drunken ones and run them all the way back, so they decided to behave and leave the old man alone.

When I first got out to Stone City the storekeeper's little daughter came up to buy three cans of corn. I hollered and asked the boss if corn was three cans for a quarter, like it was back in Shackle Island. After the customer left, the storekeeper bawled me out good, said everybody would want to buy corn for that price.

Soon after that, Mr. Thayer, one of the head men, came in and wanted a special lantern globe. He handed me a half dollar. I thought that was too much, and asked the storekeeper how much the globe was. He just answered, "Put the money in the drawer." Mr. Thayer stood there waiting for change and finally the boss came over and said, "Oh, I thought you just gave him a quarter." Then he had me to give Mr. Thayer a quarter back, and he apologized to the customer. That was the last time the boss ever talked sharp to me.

It seems like I'm getting forgetful or losing my mind one, because Dr. Johnson, the bone doctor, came in here and I plumb forgot to ask him how the old gray mule was.

Back in the old days, we sang, "Johnson Had an Old Gray Mule," so I always get a kick out of asking somebody by that name about his old gray mule. I'm still not too sick to try to get a little fun out of life, cause I never like to be a grouch, even in the hospital. The old gray mule was a cantankerous animal that even kicked the roof off the barn, so the song says. But, I guess Dr. Johnson is too young a man, anyhow, to remember the old song

The doctors now say that I'm having to stay here this long because I tried to get out of bed and fell and broke my hip, but most doctors don't know a bit more than a jack rabbit about me. Most doctors these days are too young to know anything about old gray mules or jack rabbits either for that matter, for they were both something that belong to the days of long ago.

Note: Billy the Goat has returned to Vertical Plains, Route 5, Goodlettsville, and will be recuperating there for several weeks until his hip has mended. He and his family appreciate all the cards, gifts, and visits made by his friends far and near.

A DAUGHTER'S GIFT

December 17, 1964
Goodlettsville Gazette

Billy the Goat's
Tales of Two Towns
By L. D. R.

It's almost Christmas time again, and I remember that last Christmas the only gift I requested was a subscription to the *Goodlettsville Gazette*. Well, the gift came and has brought much pleasure. However, one of the sparkling articles I enjoyed so much has been missing too long from the last several issues. Since Billy the Goat seems to be too busy to write, I shall try to fill in for him. (By the way, one of my neighbors says she only took the paper to read Billy's column.)

You've heard of the "man without a country." Well, if there were no such thing as the "country," the man this article honors today would be as useless as a corn picker in a strawberry patch. This eccentric fellow tried the city, but pressing concrete was much less exciting than swinging on Nature's grapevines or digging ol' Mother Earth for ginseng in the Spring.

Let me tell you about his first automobile. Seated proudly at the wheel one day, he decided to take a trip back to the big city to show off his vehicle. Well, he did "show off" plenty, that's for sure. As far as he was concerned, there was nobody else in town that day but him. As he made his merry way down Union Street, suddenly a cop waved at him to stop. The busy cop came over to the car and sharply chided, "Buddy, can't you see these stop lights along this street?" The instantaneous reply of this undaunted hill-habitant was also in question form. "Can't you see I'm from the country?"

he queried. Admitting defeat the cop waved him on, shouting after him, "Get on out of the way."

Years and years later, long after this fellow had learned there were such things as red lights that say "STOP" and green lights that say "GO," he made his was by bus to the capital city of our nation. This was war time and everybody was suspected of being a spy until proved otherwise. Somebody had already tipped off the G-men that this fellow who ordered hamburgers every meal on the way up—breakfast, dinner, supper—could bear watching. Anybody acting that country must be putting on an act. Therefore an FBI man met him at the bus depot and during his entire stay in Washington, there was an FBI man keeping him under close surveillance. His stay in DC was a spectacular one (at least he made a spectacle of himself everywhere he went), and on the day he left his secret was out. After intense questioning he confessed. He was no spy at all but had gone there hoping to find that silver dollar that the father of our country many years before had thrown across the Potomac. Imagine his surprise when he was told that George's silver dollar was not even thrown across the Potomac at all but across the Rappahannock in Pennsylvania! Well, the end of the Washington story is that one of these FBI men outsmarted this Tennessee hillbilly and stole the first of his six prize daughters right from under his nose, while he was looking for unretrievable silver dollars.

For nigh on to fifty years, my subject has lived on his rocky Long Hollow farm, once known as Vertical Plains. After many winters brining to him a snowcapped top, a bent back and slower step, the name of this inclining land was automatically changed to Vertical Pains.

Your narrator has climbed these hills to garnish some of the delectable fruits grown thereon. Panting behind him every step of the way, there was never any breath in me to talk. Yet he missed not a minute on the way up telling all his plans for those hills and his past failures and accomplishments thereon. Reaching the top, aching limbs called out for rest, but this amazing toreador would show me where to pick the best berries and there was no rest for the weary. Once a mad hornet from the berry vines stung me and I cried out in pain. This man of the mountains quickly came to my rescue, laid his chewing tobacco (It is good for something!) on the burning wound to draw out the poison and five minutes later all pain was gone.

Just let me say one more thing about Billy the Goat—about how rich he is. Because he has given away everything he ever had to anyone who needed or asked help, he is very, very rich. He lives by the axiom that the only thing one ever keeps is what he gives to others. When I was a child those were the days of begging and borrowing. At least once a week, some tramp stopped to beg bread or stay the night. Or else this man picked them up on his way home from work and told them there was always plenty of room. After all, there were only nine of us children, but the neighbors around who had three or four were crowded.

There's one case I especially remember: One cold nightfall Billy returned from work bringing a penniless elderly lady and her grandson. From heaven knows where they were trying to get to Carthage to attend her son's funeral. After supper, my brothers and I, ages 12 and 11 respectively, were told to ride up the road with Billy. Into each house we went and told our story—these two wayfarers had to be put on the bus the next day for Carthage. Some gave dimes, some quarters—our total collection was $3.40. Early next morning these wanderers, with warmer clothes and full stomachs, boarded a bus to complete their journey.

Some leave their children money, or houses, or land, but the heritage he will leave cannot be measured by an earthly measure nor compared to an earthly treasure.

Now I've finished my Christmas gift to him—hope he continues to send me my gift.

—Just one of the Kids

Written by Mary Onezima Ralph Bradley,
Third daughter of L. D. R.

Memories of Granddaddy . . . .

Christmas at Vertical Plains

Every year someone says it—a clerk in a department store, a college chum I meet for lunch, my hairdresser. And I know that for them it is true.

"Christmas is for children," they say. "If there aren't children there, it's no fun."

For me, however, the joy of Christmas was not children, but an adult—my maternal grandfather. His joy in Christmas and his individual interpretations of it carried the true meaning of the season for his grandchildren.

As children we knew exactly where the real Christmas was: it was at Granddaddy Ralph's house. We had fun at our own houses and with the other grandparents and aunts and uncles, but the epitome of Christmas was Granddaddy Ralph. A self-educated farmer, carpenter, writer, and jack-of-all-trades, he was quick to qualify to you that he was master of none. Perhaps he was right, but to us children that was beside the point, for we knew he had mastered Christmas.

As his nine children and their multitudes of children arrived on Christmas Eve, he'd be sitting by the fireplace chewing his tobacco and spitting into the fire. We grandchildren were intrigued by the ritual of his taking out the plug, the dexterity of his wrenching off a quid just the right size, and the methodical chewing required before his story could resume. His children lauded his talents as a carpenter, the main trade by which he'd supported his large family, but we were more impressed by his facility with a plug of tobacco. Granddaddy, the tobacco, and the stories melded together to create magic for us.

For with Granddaddy, there was always a story. The listeners could come and go throughout the day, but the stories and Granddaddy remained by the fire. In the early years, the sons-in-law were entrapped,

then the grandchildren, and finally the grandsons-in-law, all initially intrigued, then eventually bored by the garrulous old man. His adventures on the Colorado frontier were my favorite, stories of Mexicans and settlers and pioneers that made meaning out of my school history lessons.

But when gift-time arrived, Granddaddy was ready for that, too. Every year he would go to the ancient Five and Ten in their small town of Goodlettsville, Tennessee, and get gifts for all the children. The adults disdained the "junk Daddy always gets at Ruby Hitt's," but the children loved it. The junky ceramic cats, the little wooden jumping jacks, and the marbles in leather bags were our favorites far above the lovely books and clothes given by the other adults. And even after I was married, the personal nature of the gifts continued. We received a papier-mâché hound dog whose head bobbed knowingly. "Every family needs a dog," he muttered, between spits. "Now you've got one." Perhaps there wasn't quality in a material sense, but his spirit was in his gifts.

On the other hand, the gifts he got for the adults were of the finest. Never wrapped, not even packaged, they were parked on the back porch to be picked up as we left. We'd all see them as we arrived, but everyone acted as if they were invisible until after we'd all assembled in the living room to open gifts. Once everyone's gifts were opened, and that part of the festivities seemed to be ended, one of the aunts would say, "Hush! Daddy's trying to tell us something." Then he'd clear his throat, spit into his can (much to the chagrin of all the women), and say, "There are apples and oranges on the back porch. There are plenty for all of you to take a bunch. The apples are Winesap. They were hard to find this year. The oranges are those new navel ones. I never have figured out whether that's n-a-v-e-l or n-a-v-a-l and no one else seems to know either. Every time I see it written it's different. Anyway, they're good eating oranges and you need some good fruit in you after these cakes and pies and all."

Some years it was dried fruit, or tangerines, or bananas. But each carried a commentary for which everyone waited, after which they would praise Granddaddy for his delicious gifts. Then, with all the preliminaries out of the way, the fun began.

Granddaddy had been Santa for the Old Beech School Christmas parties for years, and a highlight of my childhood was when I got to go with Grandmama and Granddaddy to that party. He passed out gifts from a big bag and zeroed right in on local bullies and lazy students to put a little fear into them concerning their Christmas gift possibilities. Then he ended with a song whose words he had written himself, and every Christmas as he sang it for us, to the tune of "The Ballad of Jesse James," I could still see the 12-foot tree and all the little children gazing in awe at actually seeing the "real Santa." My pride was not only that I knew who he was when they didn't, but also that I knew that they were right—he <u>was</u> the real Santa.

Verse 1
Santa Claus is the man
Who travels through the land
And makes the children smile.
Over hills and housetops, too,
Bringing Christmas cheer to you,
And he's traveled many a mile.

Chorus
With a million tons of toys
For good little girls and boys
Who try to do right.
But the doubting little Jake
Who says Santa is a fake
Gets no presents here tonight.

Verse 2
He's the same old Santa Claus

That visited your grandpas
In the days of long ago.
Yes, children, I say such
You favor very much
Ones I visited a hundred years ago.

Verse 3
Santa's beard is getting gray
I hear some of you say.
But who can wonder why?
For nineteen hundred years
They've escaped the barber's shears;
Old Santa is never going to die.

It was the greatest Christmas song we'd ever heard, and we begged him to sing it again and again, but to no avail. One song and he was back to the fireplace, back to his stories of his early years of adventure, of people he'd known and places he'd been and lessons he'd learned. And even now, remembering the lessons he taught us through his stories—lessons about truth and friendship and justice—I realize that in my childhood, Christmas wasn't only gifts and trees and Santa. It was Granddaddy Ralph.

Christmas and Christmas memories mean something different to each person. For me, Christmas is not just for children, for I have seen it done to perfection by an elderly Tennessee carpenter. Every Christmas I'm taken back to that childhood excitement of being at home with the one-and-only, really true Santa Claus.

Lanita Bradley Boyd
Teacher/author
First grandchild of Luther and Hester Ralph
Daughter of Lawrence and Mary Onezima Ralph
Bradley

His Way

Headed towards a career in journalism in the early 1970's, it became a badge of honor to learn that among many other things my maternal grandfather was also a newspaper columnist. Maybe my genes really were aligned properly; maybe the story telling ability of Luther David Ralph had indeed skipped a generation; and maybe, *just maybe,* "Billy the Goat's Tales to Two Towns" that once graced the pages of the *Goodlettsville Gazette* could serve as a source of pride for an aspiring writer like myself.

A somewhat reluctant farmer and sometimes carpenter by trade, Luther Ralph also found time on his Vertical Plains estate in Sumner County, Tennessee, to not only write about his life's experiences, but to raise a large and promising family on Long Hollow Pike. He had gone west as a young man, sowing the seeds of youth and taking-it-all-in during stops at places like Cripple Creek, Colorado. Many of his newspaper columns came from what he saw during those western adventures and the vivid memories they inspired.

It made for good reading, as did his carpenter's bench, where creative thoughts had time to develop and mature during a normal workday. The same could even be said for his hilltop farm, far removed from the bustle of an expanding household, where a man could go to be alone with his thoughts.

Come to think of it, maybe that's why he selected the "billy goat" as his representative in print. Proud, very independent and a lover of the great outdoors—that was LDR, all right. Never one to miss a good shade tree, he also enjoyed conversation as long as it maintained a positive approach. There were good stories to be found and shared each and every day, but let negativity intrude, especially when it involved his wife of 62 years or one of his oh-so demanding daughters, and a natural born case of "stubbornness" would ensue. That's when the great outdoors would beckon and Billy the Goat would return to his hills.

Turns out he had too much to share to be bogged down with life's traumas—at least that's the way it now appears to a grandson who witnessed more than one of these family conversations during occasional visits. Writing was obviously his means of taking it beyond what normal conversation would allow and like everything else, he told it all—***his way.***

F. Martin Harmon
Journalist/author/public information officer
Seventh grandchild of Luther and Hester Ralph
Son of Frank and Evelyne Lucille Ralph Harmon

Luther David Ralph, aka "Billy the Goat"